ife Behind Glass

A Personal Account of Autism Spectrum Disorder

By Wendy Lawson

Jessica Kingsley Publishers
London and Philadelphia

Acknowledgments

My sincere thanks go to all of those who have taken the time to journey with me for a while. In particular I thank my family for loving me as I am. To Ms Smith and Ms Gahan from my Junior School in Chippenham, for your patience. To Suzette Young, my surrogate mother and mentor, thankyou! To Rob Watts who helped me so much with my writing direction. To Amanda Golding for enabling me to feel like a 'real' person. To Trice, my continuing companion whose acceptance of who I am gives me life and hope for tomorrow. This book is dedicated to all those seeking to understand and to interact with what it means to be a little bit different! Enjoy the journey.

First published in 1998
by Southern Cross University Press

Published in the United Kingdom in 2000
by Jessica Kingsley Publishers
116 Pentonville Road
London N1 9JB, UK
and

400 Market Street, Suite 400
Philadelphia, PA 19106, USA

www.jkp.com

Li...
A CIP catal...

A CIP cat...

ISBN 978 1 85302 911 0

CONTENTS

ACCEPTANCE

Life is a journey for travellers; we are all just passing
through.
However, life can be so different, for either me or you.
A word spoken in anger can wound eternally.
A word spoken in kindness, can set the hurting free.

I have set before you life or death,
Which is it that you choose?
The roads can lead you either way,
But with one road we lose.

To choose to live, take tomorrow's hand.
To choose to give, take love's fair stand.
If you desire a life that's free,
Then pay the price and follow me.

For roads can be long and weary,
When travelling alone.
But the journey's sweet, when friends we meet
Who help us find our home.

Wendy Lawson

FOREWORD

Autism is a pervasive developmental disorder that is almost always apparent from early childhood. The syndrome is characterised by profound deficits in communication and social understanding and by ritualistic and obsessional behaviours. Although associated with a range of possible causes, genetic factors are probably implicated in the majority of cases (Lord and Rutter, 1994)

The condition was first systematically described by Leo Kanner in the USA in the 1940s, but a remarkably similar account, written by Hans Asperger in Austria, appeared at much the same time (for a translation of Asperger's initial paper, see Frith, 1991). Although there continues to be some debate over the issue of differential diagnosis, most research indicates that the clinical picture and outcome of children with autism and those with Asperger Syndrome are remarkably similar (Wing, 1981). Thus, current diagnostic criteria for Asperger Syndrome, used by both the American Psychiatric Association and the World Health Organisation note the same obsessional and social-communication deficits as in autism; the distinguishing features are the presence of relatively normal cognitive skills and the lack of early language delays in individuals with Asperger Syndrome.

Although once considered to be a very rare condition, affecting only 3-4 individuals in every 10,000, recent studies have suggested much higher prevalence rates. Thus, if children within the wider "autistic spectrum" are included the prevalence may be as high as 91 per 10,000, or almost 1% of the population (Wing, 1996).

Most parents of autistic children have serious concerns about their development in the first year of life. These early anxieties tend to focus around abnormalities in communication, play or social responsiveness, or on repetitive behaviours. However, as children grow older, the pattern of their development is largely affected by the degree of cognitive impairment. Although the syndrome can occur in individuals of all levels of ability, the majority (around 70-75%) has some associated learning disabilities and around 50% have an IQ below 50. Amongst those with severe to profound cognitive impairments, few acquire useful speech and they may also exhibit more disturbed behaviours, such as aggression or self injury. Most individuals in this group will require specialist education and life-long care.

In contrast, among the 20% or so of individuals with autism or Asperger Syndrome who have an IQ within the normal range, outcome is much more variable. Most do show improvements with age, and although for some , adolescence may bring about an upsurge in problems, for others, notably those who become more aware of their difficulties, it can be a period of remarkable improvement and change (Kanner, 1973). Within this group, some individuals remain highly dependent throughout their lives; others make successful careers, they may live more or less independently, develop friendships or even (in a minority of cases) get married. Nevertheless, even amongst those who make greatest progress, their communication and social problems continue to affect many aspects of their lives, as the following account so clearly illustrates.

Patricia Howlin
Senior Lecturer in Psychology
St. Georges Hospital, London

Introduction

This is My Story

I was 42 years old when I was appropriately diagnosed with Asperger's Syndrome in August 1994. I had always known I was different from other people and "had problems" but this had been wrongly explained by a misdiagnosis of schizophrenia as a young adult and an episode of post-natal depression after the birth of my first child at 22.

Being quite academic and possessing a love for books, poetry and study, I have an insatiable appetite for knowledge. This need to understand the world around me drives me to interact with people and constantly explore their reasoning for what they do, think and feel.

Throughout my life I have been unable to identify, understand and express my emotions, and so have always felt misunderstood and alienated from those around me. Because I appear to be "different", confused and a misfit, I have been often treated as if I am either deaf or stupid.

I am neither. I simply find the world around me difficult to comprehend, and therefore my behaviour may be viewed by some as egocentric and a bit odd. Others may see me as emotionally immature, self-centred or emotionally dependent. All of these traits can certainly be true, especially when I am feeling unsure of what to expect.

But some people have given me a chance; they have believed in me. It is because of their commitment to me, to my education and to my ability to connect with what is happening around me, that I have survived.

Around nine in 1000 children will be born autistic — and many of those will have Asperger's Syndrome. Those children will become autistic adults, but they do not have to grow up feeling as if there is no place for them. With appropriate diagnosis, early intervention and subsequent training, the way can be opened for them to flourish and share their outlook on life. By understanding the hopes, dreams, strengths and weaknesses of autistic people, society can gain a deeper and rounder view of human nature.

Many people ask me what autism and Asperger's Syndrome are, and what they can expect to encounter from individuals who are autistic. This is my story. It is an attempt to explain my experience of life with Asperger's Syndrome.

This book has taken a very long time to write — I began to write it over 20 years ago. However, I believe that it could not have been written before now because we were not ready to receive its message.

Many of you will understand what autism is. For others this topic will be new. It may be surprising to learn that not all autistic people lack language skills and the ability to express themselves! In fact, many of my good friends who live with autism lead ordinary lives and do not allow their autistic disposition to hinder them from achieving their goals.

After coming to terms with what it means to be autistic, and the realisation of a failed marriage and consequent divorce, I am at last standing up to be counted.

Dr Asperger may have defined the syndrome I was born with, but I have decided his descriptions of my limitations will be the means to remove the bars from my cage — not reinforce them.

There have been dark days and depression but I hope you will find that my story is also one of hope and encouragement. I have found much meaning in my life that I hope will be valuable to all parents of autistic children, health workers and interested readers.

I hope this book will turn the light on for you, and perhaps it will be another link in the chain towards greater understanding, acceptance and respect for those of us who are "different".

Chapter 1

My World Behind Glass

One of the best ways of understanding what autism is like is to imagine yourself as a perpetual onlooker. Much of the time life is like a video, a moving film I can observe but cannot reach. The world passes in front of me shielded by glass.

On a good day, I can smell the flowers and taste the inviting aromas. What I cannot do is fully participate in the complexities of apprehension, interpretation, communication and comprehension.

According to the impressions of those around me, my experience of living with autism is like being a written sentence that is incomplete. Some have said that I remind them of a person who is not whole and who lacks the ability to operate as a complete person.

But who can say what is "complete" and what is lacking? It may be that some of us just view life differently and, therefore, actually help to make up for the "lacks" that others experience.

•

One of the key traits of Asperger's Syndrome is obsessional and compulsive behaviour, and this is certainly true of me. As far back as I can remember, I have been distracted and absorbed by repetitive sounds and movements.

I remember on my eighth birthday I received a new red bicycle with shiny silver mudguards. I was oblivious to the birthday tea and the celebrations, nor do I remember being excited about my birthday, but I do remember those mudguards!

I turned my new bicycle upside down and spun the wheels round and round and round. The light gleaming from the silver mudguards seemed to go on forever. It was so intoxicating and I felt so alive. To have that feeling interrupted by so much as a word or an action evoked extreme irritation and anger in me. I hated being disturbed or interrupted when I was involved with some repetitive action that gave me delight. I felt a sense of connection as I watched the shiny mudguards. I felt safe, almost as if I were part of the bike. It belonged to me and I to it.

This is still my experience today, only now I have come to understand that interruptions do not mean "the end"; they are only inconvenient and frustrating. Colour and shiny surfaces are just examples of mediums that connect me to life and to feeling.

In between episodes of compulsive behaviour, I yearn for calmness and constancy. When things stay the same it's easier to feel safe, to understand what is expected and to gain a sense of connection. For me, it is easier to function with routine and constancy than to process the complications such as choice and decision. I think this is because Asperger people lack the ability to discern and judge change using the same cues as non-Asperger people. Change, therefore, is very threatening, causing panic and confusion for the Asperger person.

What I do realise is that I do not see the world as others do. Most people take the routines of life and day-to-day connections for granted. The fact they can see, hear, smell, touch and relate to others is "normal". For me, these things are often painfully overwhelming, non-existent or just confusing, but when an experience or emotion is attached to some form of connecting stimuli, such as colour and fragrance, I am more likely to relate to it.

I find colour simply fascinating and it stirs all sorts of feelings in me. The stronger and brighter the colour, the more stirred up I become. My favourite colours are rich emerald green, royal blue, purple, turquoise and all the in-between shades of these colours.

My friends tell me most people do not stop and take time to notice the bright colours around them: the colour of a door they are about to open, a wall or sign that happens across their path. They don't stop and stare for ages, lost in the wonder at the "feeling" the colour evokes.

An example is the emotion stirred by freshly fallen snow on an English winter morning. I remember one particular morning, when I was coming home after working night shift at the hospital as a student nurse in Guildford, Surrey. Fresh snow had fallen during the night and my footprints were the first ones to make any impression on the frozen footpath. I stopped, afraid to move for fear of disturbing the perfection before me. I didn't want anything to change. I wondered why the colours and fragrance were so vibrant to my senses that I could "feel" them.

This intensity was juxtaposed by a feeling of emptiness at not sharing the sadness of other staff and the family of a patient who had died during the night.

I find it perfectly exciting to study a nectarine growing on the tree in my garden. The smooth almost-round shape covered in red, orange and yellow with a green splash in the middle is most exhilarating! To be able to watch them grow and develop is a miracle that never ceases to amaze me. To take half an hour to look at one does not seem strange to me — indeed it is hard to take my eyes away from the fruit even after such a length of time.

I could never understand the apparent apathy of my friends to the rich intensity and feelings in colours. I could tell they were not impressed by my "finds". Sometimes I was aware of their frustration and impatience with me, however my connections to feeling are life giving for me and colour helps me to connect.

While colours can evoke intense emotions and feelings of ecstasy, certain noises and the pitch of some sounds cause me a lot of discomfort. The buzzer on the microwave oven, children's voices, car horns, the bus bell people activate to tell the driver they want to get off, a kettle whistling ... these are just some of the sounds I find unbearable. Apparently autistic people are often prone to hypersensitive hearing.

On the other hand, tunes and music or a gentle low-pitched voice can temporarily relieve moments of fear and anxiety. You'll still catch me humming, singing, whistling and even talking out loud in an attempt to dispel confusion or unease due to change. The strategy enables me to think and calm down.

Just as sharp sounds can cause anxiety and unease, and soft ones comfort, touch and texture have a profound impact on me. I often find being touched and certain textures extremely unpleasant — for example, even in bed on a very hot night I need to wear pyjamas so that the skin on one leg does not come into contact with the skin on the other. On the odd occasions I have slept without pyjamas, I have folded the sheet so that it lies between my legs, avoiding direct contact.

During times of anxiety or loneliness, however, the softness of my leather purse, leather jacket, or the silkiness of inside coat pockets and other pieces of clothing, is very soothing. I like to run my hands through soft, furry textures.

For some people comfort can be found in a bottle of wine, good music, a good book, a good friend and a long walk, but for me soft materials, rocking to and fro, sucking the roof of my mouth, bright colours, routine and reassurance are able to calm and comfort me. Robbed of these things I am like a wild lion or a bat without its radar, and I can crash miserably!

My relationship with food and taste can also be perceived as eccentric. For reasons I don't fully understand, I like to mix and mash up my food. This is still how I like to eat at home, but driven by a desire to be like other people and eat what they do, I have learnt to enjoy most foods. It has taken me a long time and much perseverance to arrive at this point.

Growing up, mashed potato or banana were my favourite foods — the soft texture did not hurt my mouth. These were followed by baked beans, lots of gravy, and raw vegetables such as apples and carrots. I found cooked vegetables unpleasant on my tongue and the roof of my mouth — sometimes I felt like the food was choking me. Meat never really interested me and most of my meals had little, if any of it at all. Eggs could only be eaten if they had been scrambled.

I blend foods together to cope with the different textures. I like colour combinations on a plate — orange carrots, white potato, green runner beans — but the mixing disguises the textures.

"Marmalade and cheese!" my friend exclaimed in horror.

"Yes — it's even nicer with banana."

"You're not pregnant or something are you?"

My mind wondered what the "or something" meant.

•

The different perceptions of autistic children mean they are not aware of the dangers recognised by most people. Shopping centres, fun parks, schools and zoos can be very scary places because they are noisy, confusing, crowded and full of unfamiliar sights. But autistic children do not have any sense of danger when it comes to roads, oceans, rooftops or cliffs. They seem constant and non-threatening, offering quietness, calm and reassuring space — a place without interruptions and abundant with activities to occupy and satisfy the autistic child's need for sameness and repetition.

For parents of autistic children there is the constant fear of their child wandering off. As a child I was a real escape artist — Mum said I often managed to run away. With four children in the family, it must have been difficult to keep an eye on me all the time.

A Point to Ponder

I have often wondered if Asperger people are able to appreciate colour, taste, sound and texture to a higher degree than non-Asperger people? Perhaps there is a way such talents or heightened senses can be harnessed? Of course Asperger people are already benefiting from these gifts because they know the joys of such treasures, but their joy can easily be turned into frustration and anger or sadness and fear by the words of others who do not understand.

Chapter 2

Love And Feelings Are A Mystery

For me, the ordinary interactions of my daily social experiences have always been a great mystery. When I see the people around me and on television and in books interacting and expressing the desire to be in the company of others – and then compare this to my own responses and feelings – I can see that I am quite different to other people.

I find emotions interchangeable and confusing. Growing up, I was not able to distinguish between anger, fear, anxiety, frustration or disappointment. To an autistic person, kindness, affection and intimacy are confusing because they do not seem to have a purpose; sometimes it is tempting to think that maybe that is their purpose. Emotions are not concrete structures that can be seen, held or organised. They can be likened to being locked in a maze that has no exit: all paths look the same and lead to the same place. This place is very confusing and will often cause fear and even terror in an autistic person.

I could tell the difference between a comfortable feeling and an uncomfortable one, but I didn't know what to do with it. I often felt so disconnected from the world around me and was completely unaware of expected or appropriate ways of responding. From what I have read and studied, I understand that my experience is common among people with Asperger's Syndrome.

I have learnt to recognise the subtle differences between anger, frustration and disappointment, and understand why

I feel these things. By studying an individual's posture, actions, voice tone and facial expression, I can now usually work out what they are feeling. The hard work of studying the reactions of others and recognising that people respond differently to different emotions has been very beneficial to me. I now can feel fairly confident with those who know me.

When someone is receiving praise or encouragement, I have noticed that both parties usually wear a smile. Their voices are not usually loud, hands are shaken or held and eye contact is maintained. They usually stand about a metre apart.

With anger, I have observed that voices are usually louder, higher pitched, and can contain much exclamation with swearing or repetition. The angry person may talk right up close to you, their face turning red and their feet almost standing over yours. In other instances, there can be a large distance between people, waving arms and closed fists.

When emotions are more subtle and less easily defined, I find it helpful to ask the other person how they are feeling.

Communication with autistic people is difficult, especially if the individual is also intellectually disabled. It is my belief, however, that we just operate on a different level of communication and that once this is discovered, strategies for mutual understanding can be developed.

I find the written word much easier to comprehend than the spoken word. It takes me a lot longer to process conversation and work out the meaning behind the words than it does to scan the words on a written page. I think this is because I must also read the expressions on a person's face and study their body language.

Learning to listen actively has been my best teacher. It has also been the hardest lesson to learn because my natural disposition is to talk and talk about myself!

The training I received at university has been very helpful to me. In my communication studies I had to practise listening skills. When I was not listening, other students helped me to see what I was doing wrong and showed me how to constructively attend, while offering me the reassurance I needed to know that I was doing fine.

"So, Sheila. How do you think that session went?" The words left my mouth in a confident manner. There was a moment's silence – but it seemed to go on forever.

"Actually, Wendy, it felt like you had no interest in what I was saying at all!"

Her words startled me.

"Oh ... ummm ... can you please explain to me why you felt that way?"

"Look, I know we are only practising and this counselling session is not for real, but what I shared with you was still a real problem to me and yet you seemed not to care. I am feeling quite hurt at your lack of attention and interest!" I felt surprised because I had tried so hard to listen to her.

"Why did you think I was not interested in what you were saying to me?" I replied, trying to stay calm and in control.

"It was very obvious because you did not look at me throughout the session." Sheila was looking at the ground.

"So, if I look at you while we talk, you feel I am listening, but because there was little eye contact, you felt I was not interested in what you had to say?" I was finally beginning to understand what she was saying, although the concept was not new.

"Sheila, I'm really sorry you felt this way. Please be reassured that I am interested in you and in what you have to say. The problem here is one of communication. I actually hear you better when I am not looking at you! However, because this is a problem for you I would like you to be patient with me while I learn to work on my lack of eye contact."

Sheila smiled, thanked me for my honesty and said she would not take it so personally in the future. She also encouraged me to at least give the appearance of making eye contact during counselling sessions. It was explained that this could be done without necessarily looking at another person's eyes but rather attempting to look in their general direction now and then, with occasional eye contact at other times.

This advice has proven to be an enormous advantage to me and has been a great helping strategy. Although it is still easier to hear people when eye contact is avoided, I do attempt to look at them during conversation. I accept this is a social norm in Western cultures.

With people I know well and have come to trust, eye contact is not so uncomfortable, but they will never understand the battle I have gone through to be able to do this. I can understand why Aboriginal people believe eye contact destroys the soul of their ancestors!

•

The ideas of "relationships", "marriage" and "family" are all-pervasive. It seems to me that people prefer the company of others, especially when they are afraid. While I have come to accept that desire, it is not one I fully understand. I am beginning to discover what it is like to enjoy the company of someone else and not feel afraid. Sometimes I am actually able to find comfort in being together with another person. This is something I have been developing over the past ten years.

For most of my life I have lived with a sense of being different and distant from my family and those around me. To my family, I was always different because I lived in a world of my own and seemed unable to relate socially as other children did. My behaviour was just "Wendy's idiosyncrasies".

While members of my family developed their own ways of dealing with my disability, my sense of isolation and depression grew with time. I went deeper into my own world for some sense of reconciliation and self-comfort.

As the years passed, my siblings and I drifted apart because of our different lifestyles, but the general lack of understanding that we allowed to develop only made things worse.

Growing up, I was not aware of how I responded to others, nor they to me. Now I have a greater understanding of social interaction, and usually the ability to choose whether

I live in my own world or whether I join the "world" of those around me.

Even my mother could not understand my disability and disconnection and she took my inappropriate behaviour personally.

"Wendy," she would moan, "you don't care about your own mother. Why are you doing this to me?"

Mum often despaired of me but I never understood why and she never explained. Maybe I would not have sat still long enough for her to try!

For so many years my disability was never acknowledged in my family. It was just a case of an unappreciative and insensitive daughter/sister who liked to "do her own thing". Once, during a conversation, my mother said to me, "You were never normal, you probably got it from your father's side."

Got what, I wondered?

Their denial was probably a defence mechanism that enabled my family to cope. Recent studies suggest that families with a child with an Autistic Spectrum Disorder (ASD) suffer higher "stress" levels than from almost any other disorder.[1]

My father was a tall slim man who had worked in bomb disposal during the war. He had dark eyes, dark wavy hair and a reputation as a "ladies man". Mum said he was a charmer and that women always fell for his smooth ways. Although I never really understood what she had meant by this, I knew that there had been much pain in their relationship before they divorced after 28 years of marriage. I was 17 years old.

I considered him a kind man and longed to be liked and approved by him. Unfortunately, my father couldn't handle my obsession with continuity, consistency and repetition. My attempts to communicate with him were unsuccessful. He died of lung cancer before I could explain to him how I felt or what I was thinking.

The Easter vacation after his death, I stayed for a few days with my sister in the country. My youngest son, Peter, was nine at the time and he came with me to enjoy the opportunity of seeing his three male cousins again.

Although I had not spoken to my sister, Paula, of "family things" in a long time, I was interested in talking to her about the past. She was not really interested in such a conversation but she mentioned a tape that Dad had made for her before his death. I asked if I could listen to it.

"Ah ... yes you can, but remember Dad made the tape for me and I want to keep it. It's personal."

Yes, I thought, I know it's personal. I wondered why Dad never made a tape for me.

On the tape, he said he had noticed I was "different". He described me as "strange" and spoke about some occasions in my childhood. He said he had never understood me.

His words made me feel uncomfortable and hurt. Why are you saying these things to my sister, but not to me? I wondered. It was as if I was personally responsible for disappointing him.

On reflection, I think my family tried to include me in things that were happening, but kindness and affection were emotions I did not understand. I so often felt suspicious and frustrated — Why is this person talking to me? I would think. Other people seemed to be there just to interrupt and disturb me, or demand from me. I responded with withdrawal or anger.

Today, much of that misunderstanding and discomfort has gone because my family and I have taken the risk to speak about the past. I regret not being in touch emotionally with myself or with what it meant to be assertive before my father's death. I would have loved the opportunity to tell him how important he was to me and how I missed being able to communicate with him.

Recently, I have been able to talk to my family about why I appear so "distant", "scatty", "forgetful" and "unemotional". I explained it is not that I do not have emotions, but rather that I connect with them differently and for different reasons than they do.

When I explained my condition, my family was shocked and surprised. They now understand me better and I am free to be myself. Their understanding has freed me from unrealistic expectations. I do not feel pressure to perform or attempt situations on my own that would be too difficult.

Mum may not understand some of my experiences or fully comprehend what they have meant for me, but she does accept who I am today and it is good to be able to accommodate her in a bungalow in our back yard.

•

Throughout my school years, life was extremely difficult. I was constantly laughed at or teased. Sarcasm, criticism or abuse was a common experience for me but I rarely understood why. I was like an ostrich with its head in the sand – totally unaware of what was going on around me. I was confused and afraid of intimacy and genuine care.

As I approached my teenage years I began to want friends, to share my life with others. I realised that people seemed to enjoy company and appeared happier when they were not on their own. I understood friendship was valuable and I did not want to be different any more.

However, I lacked social skills and the "know how" of friendship building. Most people felt uncomfortable with my egocentric and eccentric behaviour. I wanted things to go by the rules – and my rules at that! My clumsy efforts to socialise usually ended in trauma – an experience common to most Asperger's teenagers.

One summer, my father tried to help me develop friendships. He introduced me to Brenda, a tall, attractive girl with long black hair. She smiled rather awkwardly in my direction and I could tell she was uncomfortable – she began to move away almost as soon as we were introduced.

"Say hello, Wendy," father whispered.

"Hello."

"Go and talk to her," father continued. "Make friends!" Not knowing what else to do, my gaze followed Brenda as she walked out of our kitchen. My feet followed.

She asked me lots of questions and to most of them I replied "yes". It seemed the safest thing to do; in my experience, when one answered "yes" people were happier.

Brenda was 14 years old, two years older than me. The deep red shirt she wore over her blue denim jeans intrigued me; it caught the light and held it between the creases of the material. My feet took me for a closer look and my hand reached out to touch the fabric.

"That's settled then," Brenda said, as she intercepted my hand and shook it once. Without realising it, I had agreed to go away with her for one week to a caravan park at Eggburough Power Station, in the north of England.

The arrangements were made and Brenda's mother took us both to the railway station the following week. We were to stay with Brenda's older brother and his girl friend. The train ride to Yorkshire, and then the car ride to the power station are blurs in my memory ... but I well remember the caravan park.

"These are mobile homes," said Brenda. "Come on, I'll show you where we are sleeping." My body followed her into the caravan, but my mind was trying to understand what she had meant by "mobile homes". The thought of our "home" moving while we slept did not impress me and I had a growing sense of uneasiness.

On the first night, her brother's girlfriend prepared the tea. It looked strange, and I said I was not feeling hungry. I thought the best thing to do was to go for a walk and look for trees. At least a tree is stable; it does not move and one can climb it.

Throughout the week a heavy feeling of insecurity and fear hovered over me. "Can we go home now?" I said to Brenda on the second day of our visit.

"No, we can't! What's wrong with you anyway?" My face turned away and my feet took me for another walk.

For most of the week, Brenda played with the other children in the park. They had a rope hanging off a large tree from which they swung high up over the fast-flowing stream, landing on the other side. The water looked dirty to me and this was not a game I wanted to try, but it was interesting to watch the other children, from a distance. It would have been nice to be included in their "gang" but one of the older boys had said he did not want me. Brenda liked this boy and spent most of her time with him.

The whole week was a disaster. The misery and depression I felt caused an "empty" feeling in my stomach that took away my appetite. The withdrawal from all around me was my only means of survival, and spending time close to the large tree near the stream was helpful. At night I dared not sleep in case the caravan started to move! During the day, I watched the other children, walked amongst the few remaining trees in the park or just sat in the large tree. I missed being home, being with my dog, watching my television programs and eating Mum's cooking.

My father may have thought "making friends" was a good idea but he failed to comprehend that the skills for such an exercise were far beyond me at that time. The whole arena of interaction with other human beings was foreign to me and understanding what one was supposed to do in a variety of situations just escaped me.

A Point to Ponder

It takes a special kind of commitment on behalf of "friends" to relate on a long-term basis to an autistic individual. The autistic person needs to manipulate their surroundings in order to maintain a sense of control over their environment. This will also mean that those people closely relating to the autistic person will feel manipulated and "used". Reciprocity is quite an art and one that does not come naturally if you are autistic. However, it can be learnt. Just as a child is taught to say "please" and "thank you", so too can an autistic person learn how to express appreciation, thoughtfulness or concern.

References

1. Bitsika, V., Sharpley, C., and Efremidis, B., (1997) 'The influence of gender, parental health and perceived expertise of assistance upon well-being of parents of children with autism' in *Journal of Intellectual and Developmental Disability*, Vol 22:1 pp19-28
    Burke, K., and Richdale, A., (1997) 'Study concerning needs of families and children with a diagnosis of autism, Asperger's Syndrome or Pervasive Developmental Disorder Not Otherwise Specified' Royal Melbourne Institute of Technology, Bundoora campus.

Chapter 3

My First Take On Life

On a British winter's morning, I made my arrival into the world. Befitting things to come, I did it my way – a month early and in a rush.

As if this was not enough excitement, the nursing staff were unavailable at the time; they had gone to lunch. My mother had known I was on my way but no one took her seriously. The other mums-to-be pressed their buzzers, but to no avail – I was born into the cotton blankets of my mother's bed! Eventually a nurse arrived and in damp confusion I was bundled up and carried away. Weighing four pounds, I had "sticky eyes" and was severely cross-eyed and long-sighted.

My blurred vision enhanced my first views of the world. I enjoyed having double vision and seeing dots dancing in front of my eyes. The dots became very familiar and were a constant source of comfort to me – if I squinted my eyes, I could even make them change shape and colour. As a toddler, I used this as a retreat into my own world, until at age three I was encouraged to wear glasses.

I don't remember my eyes troubling me but they must have been a source of concern for my parents. The prescription glasses helped correct both my squint and long vision. It was great to be able to see more clearly but also very confusing. I had enjoyed playing with the round dots dancing before my eyes. I could lose myself with them and feel content as colours and sparkles merged into each other before me.

As far as I was concerned, the glasses weighed heavily on my nose, hurt the backs of my ears, and sent the dots away! The only way I could make them come back was to squint towards the light and take my glasses off. Mum was always at me to put them back on and unscrew my nose.

"Wendy, put your glasses back on! You do want to have straight eyes, don't you?" I wasn't so sure. I could not imagine what she was talking about. Those glasses were the "enemy" for some time.

When I was sixteen months old, my little sister was born. She was lovely: blond hair, green eyes and very responsive. While she reached out for cuddles, my arms hung firmly by my side. All the aunts and uncles said how beautiful she was and many photographs were taken of her. I was not so cooperative and would not smile on command! I can remember dancing around in circles and being fascinated by my shadow, but I certainly did not understand the concept of posing for the camera.

"Stand still now ... that's my girl, watch the birdie," they would say. All the time I was thinking: What birdie? I can't see any birdie!

Seven months after my second birthday, along came twins: a boy and a girl. Unfortunately, they were born eight weeks early and the boy died before he could be baptised. This meant he did not qualify for a church burial.

Dad punched the doctor on the nose after the delivery because he believed he was negligent. Then, after being told that his son could not be buried, he made a vow: for as long as he lived, God and religion would have no place in his life.

21

My little brother was placed in a homemade box and put in the bath at home — the coldest place. Apparently as soon as someone else in the town died he could be buried too.

During this time a great grief and heaviness settled over our home. I did not know the feeling then — I just knew that everything seemed grey and the music had stopped altogether.

I think I knew the bathroom was out of bounds, but I went into it anyway. I remember wishing it was me in the box and not my dead baby brother. I was the one everyone seemed to be angry with so maybe if I went away their anger would stop.

Three days later he was buried. No one went to the funeral and to this day Mum hasn't visited the grave. It must be quite difficult to cope with but I am not sure denial is the best way ... however, it appears that this is the way my family chooses to deal with a number of painful situations.

In my early years I lived near the sea on the south east coast of England, where the weather is often stormy and wet. At two years old, I preferred sitting under the table during a storm to the comfort of my mother's lap. My sisters were also afraid during the storms but they stayed closer to mum. Under the table I had my coloured blocks and could spend hours just building them up and taking them down again, or simply sitting with my knees up under my chin, rocking myself.

With four children my mother was kept very busy. This was fine because it gave me more time to lose myself in our garden, or in the sounds of the seagulls and the ocean.

I had an overwhelming desire to get to the water beyond our home but was imprisoned by the four-barred gate that kept me in the garden. Mother didn't mind me being outside because inside I was like a tornado, always running somewhere or nowhere. I loved playing with the sand and the gravel on the ground around my home.

I remember one time I managed to escape. The ocean sounds wooed me and the wind whistled about my ears as I turned the corner from our sleepy side street and out onto the main road. It was unusually windy, but that didn't trouble me. I just loved the sea. It made me feel safe; it was comforting and was always there.

I walked to the sea and watched the grey and green shades of the waves change as the clouds moved across the skies. It was a chilly autumn day with not much sunlight left, and the wind had a bite to it that I hardly noticed. I walked, hopped and ran along the walkway that patrolled the cliff tops.

It was a straight walk, but a long one. It took me an hour to reach my destination and on arrival I stood for a while and stared far out to sea. Just being near it, hearing the ocean move back and forth, made me feel good. Eventually I parked myself upon a sand dune and continued to gaze into the foaming, grey-green waters. I wondered what would happen if I walked on the water; I had often seen sea birds fly down and land on it. They looked so at home on the sea.

As I approached the sandy shore I noticed how calmly the water washed over the grains of sand and pulled them back into the sea as it retreated. The movement of constant washing, pushing forward and retrieval fascinated me and I could watch it for hours.

I had my best new black shoes on and Mum had told me not to get them wet ... it's funny to think of it now, but it never occurred to me to take my socks and shoes off!. I don't know how long I sat on that dune, mesmerised by the incoming waves of the evening tide. I felt life was different beside the sea: there were no demanding voices, no instructions to follow, no commands to obey, no competition or fights with my sisters over chairs. There were no limitations, and I did not want that feeling to stop.

In the distance I heard voices calling my name. Reluctantly I stood up and looked around. My neighbour, Jenny, was standing on the steps at the foot of the cliff.

"Wendy, don't move, stay where you are. I'm coming over to get you!" Her words echoed in the wind and surprised me. I had no intentions of moving – I was very happy where I was!

Jenny walked over the damp remaining seashore and picked me up. I had not noticed that while I was sitting there, the tide had come in and my isolated sand dune was now the only sand visible above sea level.

I always needed to be on the move. Even when I was made to sit still on a chair, I had to rock it. If I sat on the floor, I needed to rock myself and suck the roof of my mouth – the rhythm and the movement meant I was alive and kept the music going. I think I believed that if I ended the movement, then that would be the end of me.

Later, when my two sisters and I shared a double bed in a room with flowers on the curtains, they would poke me and tell me to be still because they wanted to sleep. With the three of us in a double bed, I could not escape them so I placed the sheets between my legs and theirs and ran the softness through my fingers and toes. I would always suck the roof of my mouth and enjoy the sensation of knowing that I was there.

From a young age I was plagued with rheumatism. Sometimes the pain in my legs was so bad that it seemed to permeate the rest of my body. I could barely walk to my parent's room, where Mum would rub my knees, give me aspirin and let me fall asleep in her bed.

Although the walk to her room sometimes seemed fraught with danger, and the pain in my legs so bad that I couldn't move too quickly, I was afraid to turn on the light; at night the lights were to be off. Mum, Mum ... please wake up and open the door, I would think, my leg hurts so much. I wanted my mother to know I was there but the thought of waking her scared me. This meant my parents would find me standing outside their door in the mornings — sometimes I had been there for hours!

So many times I could not tell them what I wanted. I do not know what it was I feared, but it was always a hard decision to open their bedroom door and go in. When I did go in, and Mum would massage my knee, my mind would whisper: Please push down a little harder. The firm touch of her hand seemed to lessen the pain but the feel of her body so close to me was uncomfortable. For several years aspirin was a good friend, and I took comfort in the taste of the large white pills.

When I was four years old, we moved inland to Grandmother's house — an old house that I remember well. My mother, her five sisters and one brother had spent much of their childhood growing up in there, and it was full of family photos, memorabilia, and lots of love.

The large, grey stone walls of Selwyn Cottage were stained with old age and had survived the wind and rain of almost two centuries. One could get to the living room from the front door that exited straight onto the main road. At the back of the house, through the kitchen and to the side of the toilet that had a wooden seat, ran the slipway leading to a side street and on towards an oval where children played soccer.

I loved that oval. It encompassed a large green that played host to many fun fairs, family picnics and childish games. One summer, I wandered beyond the green and along the stream that ran beside it. With me were my homemade fishing net (made from a pair of stockings and a short bamboo cane) and a jam jar with a carry strap made from an old bootlace. I set out to catch minnows or frog's spawn to transfer into a fish bowl.

It was with great care and concentration that I dragged my net through the trickling waters of the bubbling brook. To my utter delight, I saw a section of calm water with frog's pawn and reached over to collect it. Suddenly my net was being flapped and pushed about in the darker waters. I lifted it up and drew it towards me. There, half in and half dangling over the edge of my net was a metre-long grass snake — with a frog in its mouth!

What a catch! I was ecstatic and tried desperately to contain them in the net, but when I pulled it in there were only a few pieces of waterweed draining in the bottom.

"Oh sure, Wendy, you almost had a snake to bring home ... pull the other one, it's got bells on," laughed my sisters and cousins. I never understood what they meant by that but I did understand they didn't believe me. It hurt so much. Why was I never taken seriously? Why was it so hard to be believed or to feel the taste of encouragement when I actually achieved something?

Grandma was different. I always felt accepted and welcomed by her. I knew she was old but she often smiled at me or patted me on the head. Sometimes she even let me sit on her lap and feel the soft material of her frock against my face.

We lived at Grandmother's house for one year, sharing accommodation with her, my aunt, uncle, and my twin cousins. My favourite and most familiar room was the attic. I was often confined there because I suffered with ear and tonsil infections, and in those days it was considered best to put the child to bed and keep them away from others.

During those days in bed I was expected to amuse myself with various colouring books and puzzles. I still cannot understand how such activities can be enjoyed! For me, spinning my coloured top and listening to its whirly sound, which went up and down depending on how fast I turned the handle, was preferable.

Not that using crayons was boring. The bright colours fascinated me, but I was never very good at keeping within the lines. With a clear sheet of paper and some wax crayons, my excitement knew no bounds! Wax crayons are wonderful; you can rub them over the paper and then make tracks over the top with your fingernails or some other sharp object. The patterns that can be made are endless.

27

Although I was unable to relate to other children (or even most other people, whatever their age) with animals it was different. I felt a definite connection to my beloved cat, given to me by grandmother on my fifth birthday. His name was Sandy, like the beach.

In order to maintain the feelings I experienced with Sandy, I imitated his behaviour. Lapping milk from a saucer felt good. I could get right down close to the floor and close to Sandy. We were best friends and he always seemed to want to be with me.

Chapter 4

School Intrudes

When I was five and still living at Grandmother's place the inevitable happened – I was expected to go to school. All I can remember about my first day is that the boy in front of me vomited and this frightened me. I did not want to go back to the school again and every time my parents tried to make me go I became uncontrollable. They decided to keep me home and try again later after we had moved away from grandmother's place.

We moved to Chippenham in Wiltshire just after my fifth birthday. Sandy was my constant companion and we shared the joy of living. In September of the same year, another attempt was made to send me to school.

Faster, faster ... my heart was pounding as my shoe-shod feet ran around the vast playground. The bitumen floor of the school playground intrigued me and I noticed that as I ran it seemed to run with me. At play times, I ran and ran and ran, giggling out loud as I did so.

After being at school for only two days, a tall woman with grey curly hair yelled at me to stop. She told me that I was in the boy's play area where girls were not allowed. I did not know that the girls and boys had separate areas and because I could not tell the difference, I stopped running. It never occurred to me to ask a teacher or fellow student.

From that day on, for several years, I did not run any more in the playground. Instead I sat on the floor and rocked myself, or hung off the railings that surrounded the playground and watched the world go by. I held on to both the knowledge that the railings would not always contain me, and the hope of being in another place. I watched the people walking past on the opposite side of the road.

There were odd occasions at school when I seemed to know things about other people before they did. One day when two children were skipping rope and the game was getting intense, I knew that one child would fall down – I had hardly seen the thought when it happened. I know this could easily be coincidence, but it happened many times. Sometimes I would dream of a place, in great detail, and then experience that very same place at some future time.

In many ways, I felt my sensory perception was superior to that of my peers. I had the ability to hear noise before they did, which meant that I could tell when the school bus was approaching before others could hear it. Noises seemed so much louder for me, and I had to move away from conversation at times because the noise hurt my ears. It was easy for me to move into a state of sensory overload and when this happened, it was always difficult to stay among people.

My family moved several times, but I hardly seemed to notice. By the time I was eight years old, I still couldn't read. I remember one teacher saying that I was "educationally subnormal". It made me think of a submarine and I thought maybe the teacher had listened in on one of my games.

Other children called me "crazy" or "mad" and some didn't like to play with me.

"So you're Wendy, are you?" The boy put his face right up against mine and pushed his lips out to one side. It reminded me of the look a tortoise has just before it bites into the lettuce leaf. I stood still, unsure of what to say. He repeated his question and signalled for the other children to draw closer. "Well, are you or not?" Not knowing how to respond, I said nothing. The boy uttered some other comment and then the bell went for end of recess.

I often played deaf or dumb. I learnt that this behaviour bore a measure of success and I employed it often.

When someone was talking to me or reading a story in class, I found it difficult to concentrate on what they were saying. Sometimes I laughed when other children did not and at other times I would miss the joke completely. It seemed preferable to stay withdrawn and not enter into conversation at all if possible. Avoiding conversation meant staying out of trouble. This presented me with constant conflict because talking helped me understand situations and was an enjoyable pastime.

Mostly, I learnt things by actually doing them. When I received my new red bicycle I already knew how to ride it. I had taught myself how to ride by practising on mother's bike (against her knowledge, of course).

One afternoon the bicycle and I went for a long ride. We were following a big double-decker red bus and as it turned at a T-junction, so did we. I forgot to look and see if any more traffic was coming before I turned; I was just intent on following the big red bus. A car coming in the opposite direction hit me at around 30 miles per hour.

My bike went one direction and I went another. After flying through the air a short distance, I fell and landed on the kerb of the pavement, momentarily knocking myself out. At the hospital they said I had a nasty bump on my head, but I was fine to go home. My bicycle was not so lucky and I never saw it again.

I do not remember my parents being angry with me over the incident with my bicycle. They did not sit me down to talk about the rules of the road. It just became yet another incident that was not talked about, and for my ninth birthday, I was given a colouring book and a pack of crayons.

When my bicycle did not return from the hospital I truly assumed it had been kept away from me so that I could not break it again. It was a form of punishment because I had been bad. My parents' lack of explanation only reinforced my belief about myself and withdrawal into my own world appeared to be the only thing to do.

"Wendy, Wendy, answer the question please!" Ms Smith's words broke through my thoughts and brought me back to the maths class. My chair came to a standstill, my legs ceased to move and the class waited for my reply.

"Emma could answer the question better than me, Ms Smith." I knew that this was the truth because Emma always answered the questions.

"That may be the case, Wendy, but I want you to answer it."

"Oh, I cannot answer the question, Ms Smith." These words were also true, and I felt no sense of alarm.

"You will stay behind and write the answer out for me, Wendy, and maybe you will pay more attention in the future." Ms Smith's words made no sense to me. I was paying attention, I thought. I was paying attention to the tree outside the window. Its leaves were all shiny in the sunlight.

Another teacher explained that "paying attention" meant to give your thoughts and your time to listen and look at something. It was not that I lacked the ability to understand events and situations, but rather that the explanations of others were incomplete!

Numbers and figures were always a mystery to me and it made my brain sore to try to understand them. This meant that it was always more difficult to attend to the teacher when we did maths.

"Wendy, why are you counting with your fingers?" asked Jane. What a silly question, I thought. It's easier to use my fingers than my toes! The problem was that my fingers were inadequate as a counting source and when the numbers exceeded what could be contained in my head, I just gave up.

"Day dreaming" was my favourite pastime. It was very rewarding and not complicated . Some might say that "day dreaming" is the wrong term for it because that implies using one's imagination. Asperger people are not supposed to have an imagination! My thoughts on this matter differ somewhat from the literature. Bright colours, softness and different shades of lighting could capture my "imagination" for hours.

Bath time, for instance, presented a wonderful dreamscape. "Wendy, you have not washed yourself, have you?"

"Mum, see how round the bubbles are. Just look at the colours!" It was wonderful to rub the soap over my hands and then blow gently through the hole that my fingers made. The bubbles also felt soft as they landed on me before popping. The sad thing was that after awhile they would go away. Why does everything always change?

One day, in the autumn of my ninth year, I was on my way home from school when I noticed a man who seemed to be staring at me. It was 4.30 in the afternoon. The man came towards me and began to talk to me. He was telling me something, but I did not understand what he was saying. We were in the oval near some blackberry bushes. It was mid-autumn and quite cool. He moved closer and put his arm out to stop me from passing by. I didn't want his arm to touch me and so I stopped walking and stood still.

I remember looking at my feet and thinking about the time (I wanted to get home because *Champion The Wonder Horse* came on TV at 5 o'clock). I was aware that the man was asking me questions. He mentioned a boy named Ben, a friend I went to school with, and said that Ben was his son. Ben was one of the boys who bothered to talk to me and did not appear to mind my company. The man, probably around 30 years old, asked me to do things that seemed strange to me. I wanted to go home. Eventually, after urinating in front of me the man let me go.

Strangely, I did not feel afraid or in danger. I thought that this was an odd thing to do, especially as I had been told numerous times that the toilet in the bathroom was the only place for this to happen. When I had wet my pants my mother was unhappy with me.

For several days after this the man met me on my walk across the oval. About a week or so later, he took me to his house. No one else was home. I worried that it was 5 o'clock and my program was on, but didn't know how to get away from him.

The man's house was dark and smelt musty — there was lots of washing up in the sink and it all looked rather untidy. Someone should clear up, I thought, as my hands collected some dirty cups from the sitting room.

"Leave those things and come here." My body moved over to where the man stood.

"Why are the curtains closed?" I asked, the words echoing my confusion. "Everyone knows that you don't close the curtains in the daytime."

The man signalled for me to come closer to him. While standing still, he took my clothes off.

"It's too early for bed and my programs are on," I said.

"This is a special time, just for us," the man said. "When we have finished you can have a ride on my motor scooter."

I don't remember feeling the pain but I do remember the blood on my underpants because it dried and stuck to my bottom.

This man took me to his home on several occasions. I don't know why I didn't say no, or why I didn't tell my parents. I think it had something to do with him being a grown-up and me being a child. It felt good to have someone's attention, even though the things he did with me felt strange. Somehow I knew my behaviour was inappropriate, but I did not know why. I did know that children did what grown-ups told them to do.

Perhaps this man realised I did not understand what was happening to me? All that I can remember thinking was that it was important to do as I was told. I haven't any memory of how I felt except that I was afraid to disobey him. Did my being different make me an easy target for this man's abuse? Even today when I think about that time in my life, I feel nothing. Maybe my experience is a common one and can be likened to that of other children.

Although devoid of emotion concerning the abuse I encountered at the hands of this man, I was very uncomfortable living in the same town as him. I was so sure all the people knew what was happening to me. I worried that other people would want me to go with them. I did not want to do this any more and prayed to God to help me escape.

In the July before my tenth birthday, my left knee became very painful and swollen. At first Mum thought my complaints were due to "growing pains", and gave me some aspirin and sent me to school. The next day my leg was still very sore and she took me to the doctor. He thought there might be fluid on my kneecap and suggested that rest might help. If there was no change, then he would drain the fluid off.

The pain increased and became unbearable. At school I refused to jump in a physical education class but the teacher did not believe that it was because my leg was too painful. At break time, I asked a friend, Gillian, if she would take me home on her pushbike. It was an awkward and painful exercise, but one that probably saved my life.

My mother put me to bed, with more aspirin and a hot water bottle. The next day, my temperature was very high and I was delirious with fever and pain. Even the thought of having my beloved cat Sandy on my bed was too much.

The doctor came to see me. Apparently he was very concerned and suggested I go into Frogwell hospital, in Chippenham. He suspected rheumatic fever. For the following week I ate bananas, when I ate at all, and drank small amounts of milk. After the results of the blood tests came back, it was recognised that I did not have rheumatic fever, but Osteomyelitis of my left tibia. I needed an urgent operation to save both my leg and my life, and was transferred to the Bath and Wessex Orthopaedic Hospital.

At any other time an ambulance ride through the red traffic lights of Chippenham would have been a real treat, however awareness of my surroundings and the reality of the situation escaped me. I slipped into unconsciousness.

"Your daughter is a very sick little girl," the surgeon told my parents. "I must amputate her leg in order to save her life."

Father asked for a few minutes to think about this.

"If you take off her leg, then you are taking away her life. Please is there no other way?" he pleaded. This doctor had a daughter with the same name as me and we even shared the same surname. Whether this had any bearing on his decision or not is hard to say, but my parents believed that it did.

The doctor agreed to operate and try to remove the diseased tissue and drain the bone abscess. He warned my parents that this may not be successful and that amputation may still be on the agenda.

I don't remember contracting a secondary infection of pneumonia or being in a coma for three weeks after the operation. I do remember waking up in a strange place and hearing two nurses discussing a party that they and their boyfriends had been to the night before.

"Who are you?" I asked.

"Don't worry about anything," one of them said. "You're fine." With those nonsensical words I drifted back into a deep sleep.

The next time I awoke, the nurse was there with some fresh bandages and some thick brownish-grey cream. The cream was kaolin; it was warm and was for wrapping around my chest. They said later that it would help to clear my lungs and aid my breathing. Within a few days, I was moved into D ward, the main one. It housed both boys and girls between the ages of nine and 15.

Most of those in D ward were long-term orthopaedic patients. This was their home and any newcomer was treated with suspicion. I felt very much alone.

"Why is this cast on my leg?" I asked the sister. "It is preventing my knee from bending.

"Exactly dear, we don't *want* your leg to bend." I didn't understand why I had to keep my leg straight, and although the nurses were very kind to me, it was many years before I was to understand what happened to me and why.

After a few weeks, it felt like my niche had been found. Doing little jobs for patients and nurses gave me a sense of importance, and being busily involved with the ward routine made me happy.

"Janet it's your turn now. Sit on my lap but hold on tight," I instructed one of the new patients. The corridors in between the wards and other departments were separated by plastic doors that opened when pushed. It was with great delight that I wheelchaired passengers on corridor tours at high speed! I could give free rides on my lap in my wheelchair to any mobile patient and I could pack a steriliser drum to perfection.

Visiting times upset hospital routine and were seen, by some nursing staff, as an interruption. For me this was a welcome interruption; the times when I did not have any visitors of my own, I delighted in sharing the visitors of other patients.

Meal times were a bit traumatic because it was the rule that all food, even cauliflower, had to be eaten. I was adept at slipping the unwanted vegetable into a paper bag for visitors to take away.

I would have liked to have visitors of my own and often stood at the ward entry at visiting times, hoping that someone would come. In almost 12 months, my father visited only twice. My mother said he hated hospitals because of the war — to him, hospitals always smelt of death. I did not know what death smelt like, but I knew that I must have that smell on me because otherwise father would come to see me.

I think I knew I was different, but I didn't know why. My world was a rich one, full of colour and music that seemed to splash over and around me where ever I walked. I thought everyone saw things the same way I did, but my behaviour seemed to make people angry or cause them to distance themselves from me.

I came to believe this was the case because I could never keep friends with anyone for very long. At first, other children seemed keen to see my dog or cat, visit my home, even to play games with me. However, few stayed for very long and even fewer repeated the exercise. I never understood why they did not want to be with me. Sometimes at school, especially during my early teens, I formed strong attachments to certain girls, following them everywhere just to be close to them.

The tone of someone's voice or the shape of their smile could lull me. Sometimes it was simply the length of their hair that attracted me and how it shone when the sun's light touched it. Certain people fascinated me, but they were few and far between. Unfortunately, my fascination and need to be close to certain people was not shared by the individual concerned and I was often asked to go away.

In the hospital, the nurses had been different. They tried to reach me and capture my attention; their acceptance and pleasure were high on my agenda. I became their little helper, performing a number of minor chores, but if one of them came too close to me I'd freeze. Sometimes a nurse would try to hug me or tickle me. This just sent me into a panic attack and I'd madly suck the roof of my mouth or reach for the sheets to wrap around me.

I did not understand why I was afraid of touch but now I think it just caused lots of sensations that were overwhelming for me. It also called for some form of response, which meant having to make a decision. Decisions were confusing for me and it was easier to play it safe and stay with what was familiar.

At the same time, I wished I could be hugged or touched without it confusing me. I had observed the other patients being tickled and hugged by the nurses and it seemed to make them happy.

I never really celebrated my tenth birthday in D ward. The nurses organised a cup cake with a large white candle in the middle of it, but I withdrew beneath the bed covers as they approached. I lay quite still as if I were asleep, and stayed that way until they gave up trying to obtain a response from me.

There was such a battle going on inside my head. I wanted to respond, to laugh and clap with them, but I was terrified. All I could do was withdraw. It must have been so frustrating for the nursing staff and the other patients involved – they probably thought I was being very silly and totally unappreciative. Yet how could I explain to them something that I did not even understand myself?

Nights in hospital were very traumatic. I slept for only short amounts of time. Many hours were spent screaming inside and wanting the nurses to come and put the lights back on, but I never made any sounds. I soaked my pillows with tears, but no noise, no noise.

The shadows frightened me, and all noises seemed so very loud. In the daytime, it was different because I was busily occupied with very important duties. We had visiting teachers but I managed to learn very little in the way of academic studies!

As the months passed, it was decided that I needed to sit for the "eleven plus" exam. This exam has been abolished in England now, but in September 1962 it was the exam all students attempted. It was to streamline them for secondary or grammar schools.

I was accompanied into a small room not far from Sister's office. It had only one desk and one chair in it, plus a loud ticking clock on the wall directly opposite where I sat. I was given a pencil and several sheets of paper and told it was important to my education that I concentrate and work to the best of my ability. Whatever "important to my education" meant, being in that office with those bits of paper did not feel very important to me.

I drew on the paper, played "noughts and crosses" and felt very anxious – I had told one of the nurses earlier that I would roll some bandages for her and I felt that really *was* important.

•

A Point to Ponder

Maybe if the exam had been explained to me and I had been told to read the information sheet accompanying the writing paper, I might have attempted to answer the questions. It would have been very helpful if the exam had been broken down into smaller chunks of information so that I could have worked without being overwhelmed by so many words all lumped together. This did not happen and neither did the "eleven plus" exam for me!

Chapter 5

A Bumpy Road To Recovery

At the age of eleven, I was discharged from the hospital with my left leg in a calliper and a walking stick to support me, and I learnt to walk again.

Not long after coming out of hospital, my family bought me a red-haired ginger mongrel dog that I named Rusty. Rusty was just six weeks old but we became inseparable and I taught her obedience. We often had adventures together and soon learnt to understand one another. To bark like a dog seemed perfectly normal to me and this activity could be shared with Rusty. It made me quite happy!

I have many good memories of the feel of a fluffy, furry coat against my fingers. Even today it's hard to resist the temptation to run my fingers through my cat's fur and lose myself in the feeling.

•

During the spring of 1965 I underwent painful surgery in Frenchay Hospital, in Bristol, for skin grafts to my left leg. I was 13 years old and Father thought it would be a good idea to cover the ugly scars that previous operations had left.

I liked the idea of going into hospital but hated the thought of anaesthetics and more pain. However, it was something Dad wanted and all I wanted was for him to be pleased with me.

On the day of my admission, Mum dressed me nicely for the doctors. I wore a tartan wool and cotton pinafore dress with a pleated skirt, and large black buttons on the shoulders that allowed me to get in and out of it. I didn't mind the dress, but since I usually wore jeans and a long sleeved shirt, it made me feel a little more exposed, though at the same time more grown up.

After the initial examination, the doctors said they would put me on bed rest to encourage the fatty tissue around my leg muscles to relax. They could then draw this up and over the scared tissue. I did not know if this was a good idea or not but cooperated with the plan and stayed in bed.

During the afternoon of the first day I was reaching over to my locker when I knocked over the tissue box. I did not know what to do so I just waited. After a short while I tried to lean out of bed and pick it up but the box was out of reach. When a nurse came past I asked her if she would pick it up for me.

"What did your last slave die of?" was her reply. "What's wrong with your back?" Her words pierced me like a knife; I pulled the sheet up over my head and cried. They told me to stay in bed, I am not allowed to get up, I thought. I wanted to go home.

But going home was not on the agenda. After a week the doctors again examined my leg and decided that the idea of using my calf muscle was not working. Instead they believed it would be better to raise a tube pedicle, using the fatty tissue from the "puppy fat" around my tummy. I did not understand the concept and was in no way prepared for what was to follow!

I was told that the skin grafting would take up to three months and that they were going to use some skin from my tummy. The doctor tickled me there and made a joke about my extra layer. I thought this meant I had some extra skin there that could be cut off and used to fill in the hole in my leg. The following day the nurse prepared me for surgery.

Back in the ward after the operation I couldn't stop whatever took over me, and my body heaved over the kidney bowl that the nurse held under my chin. The airway came out of my mouth, along with the clear yellow fluid of the anaesthetic. This vomiting continued throughout the evening.

"Nurse, can I have some orange juice?" As I spoke the words my lips seemed to cling together. My mouth was so dry and I was desperately thirsty.

"When was the last time you were sick love?" came her reply.

"I'm still sick."

"Do you feel like throwing up now?" This was an expression I understood; my sisters had used it when they vomited.

"No, I haven't thrown up for over three hours."

This was apparently a good answer because the nurse brought me some orange cordial with ice. As she was helping me sit up I noticed my tummy and the top of my leg were sore.

"Why do I have all this padding around my leg and tummy?" A simple question, really, especially in the light of my belief that it was only the middle part of my leg that was going to be operated on.

She explained that the doctor had raised a tube pedicle on my tummy and that this would become the skin graft that would cover the scar on my leg. She also explained that skin had been taken from the top of my leg to cover the exposed areas of my tummy. A feeling of shock and confusion settled into the pit of my stomach, and I realised they had not filled in the scar on my leg yet. I would have to go through this all over again!

Maybe the doctors had tried to explain the procedure to me, or perhaps they thought it was too complicated a task and decided to take each event as it happened? What I *am* sure of is that I did not understand what was happening, and felt lied to and cheated. I decided those doctors and nurses could not be trusted and withdrawal into my own world again was my only option.

"Not hungry today, Wendy?" asked the nurse.

"My tummy feels very sore."

"Staff is coming to change your dressing after lunch, so if you do not eat your lunch now you will have to wait until teatime." My head turned over on my pillow and my mind wondered how much longer the soreness in my tummy would last.

"Wendy, your tummy does not smell very nice. Has it been like this for very long?" asked Staff as she changed my dressing. "I want Sister to take a look." Sister didn't like the look of it either. She took a swab and called the doctor.

Over the next three days the nurses were very interested in me and kept looking at my tummy. It was two weeks since the first operation and it seemed that my wound was infected — when the result from the swab came back, it was panic stations!

"Wendy, we have to take you down to the theatre," Staff said. "This is something we have to do because there is a nasty infection in your wound and it must be scraped out. Don't worry about the fact that you have eaten. They will give you a stomach pump."

When I awoke I realised my bed was in a different place. The wonderful thing was there was no "sick" feeling in my stomach — in fact, my whole body felt so fit and alive. Whatever they had given me was making me feel terrific!

Gas gangrene was the name of the infection that had made my stomach so sore. Most likely it was transferred by cross-infection from the apron of the nurse who came over from the Burns Unit. It was not an uncommon result of bad burns. I did not know how close to death I had been. The infection had been active in my body for a week before it was recognised. The medical book says that gas gangrene is fatal within forty-eight hours!

The side ward where they housed me was my home for 10 days. Everything coming into the ward had to be sterile or protected from me. At least this was what I thought. All the nurses wore gowns and hats and all of my books and necessary equipment were to be destroyed after use. My confinement felt like a punishment and it was difficult to understand. The anti-gangrene injections were painful, but not as painful as my imprisonment. My recovery was speedy though, and the infection soon went away. What remained on my body were the scars from the scraped infected skin around my tummy – and they remain with me today.

During the following two years my pedicle graft took root and became a successful addition to my left leg. It filled in the hole nicely and can be observed as a small hill just below my left knee!

•

In the hospital, I met a nurse who took a particular interest in me. Lesley walked with me, sang to me and shared her lunch with me. I found her kindness very uncomfortable, but her genuine, gentle voice wooed me and drew me to her.

Thankfully she was not physically intimidating towards me. Instead she chose to give me tasks to do for her, like rolling bandages and restocking the sterile packs to go to central sterilising. If I made mistakes she did not get mad at me, shout or take the task away, but tried to teach me, step by step, how to do it properly. Thirty years later, she is still one of the most significant people in my life.

Lesley was one of the very few people to show a belief in me as a person, and she was the first to help me want to risk the pain of revealing myself and allowing love to reach me. The superficial exterior I projected to those around me did not fool this lady and she let me know that I was acceptable and lovable, just the way I was. The value of human life is not something that can be measured, but I had not considered myself valuable. For the first time, someone helped me change my thinking, treated me as worthwhile, and started something new in my life.

49

Lesley introduced me to God and told me He loved me and listened to my prayers. The concept of a loving God had always appealed to me, but I thought I was probably too bad for Him to notice. If Lesley said God cared though, then He must, because she would not lie to me.

I felt I had someone to talk to at any time and Lesley assured me that God always listened. As a young child I had gone to Sunday school on occasions and had always been fascinated by the Madonna and child stained glass window. I loved the colours in it and in the other windows in the church.

Chapter 6

Teenage Dreams And Fears

About the time I came home from hospital in Bath, my parents bought a new black and white television. I was captivated and "the box" became a large part of my evening activity. Looking back now, I can see that it was a lifesaver. I copied the characters from the American adventure programs, even taking on their accents.

By becoming an adventure hero I hoped to gain an acceptable identity. With the hero's identity, I would perform for people – I dearly wanted to be more popular. I could play the clown or the beggar, act educated or dumb, always using someone else's identity and not my own. The real "me" was kept to myself as it was not acceptable.

Sometimes performing was helpful in my social interaction with others and enabled me to feel both human and part of "the gang". There was a cost though: Wendy went underground and continued to avoid facing the reality of emotional pain and disability.

I was often confused and my sense of "self" was very muddled and frightening. I could go to the local shop and then forget why I was there. I got lost easily and even forgot my own name. Some days it was too difficult to make even the smallest of decisions, such as whether to eat one sandwich or two.

•

During my teenage years, my dog Rusty was my most loyal companion and we explored life together as only trusted friends know how.

We would climb through my bedroom window and down over the roof to the main road. One of our favourite places was the allotment across the road, where we could touch the petals of various flavouring shrubs and daisies, eat peas in their pods and play hide-and-seek among the vegetables.

"Come on, Rusty, you can do it." As I helped her climb through our bedroom window it never occurred to me that there might be things that Rusty and I could not do! Lassie was my favourite television character and there wasn't anything that dog could not do — and if she could do it, then my dog could too.

Rusty was faithful, loyal and dependable; she never changed. We understood one another, even without words. She demanded nothing from me except my acceptance and availability.

One crisp autumn evening, when Rusty was three years old and "in season", she escaped through the back door when I took out the rubbish. It was already dusk and father had said that if she got pregnant he would shoot her. Gripped by pain and fear, I put my shoes on and tried to creep out of the house, but my father saw me and asked where I was going. The look on my face told the story and he beat me to the back door.

I tried to scream, but no words came. Instead I beat on his chest and tried to stop him. My efforts were in vain and I crumbled to the floor like a tower of cards, but as soon as the door slammed behind him, I gathered myself and ran out into the failing sunlight. For three hours I walked across fields, roads and more fields. It was so dark I could not see where I was going, and on reflection it is amazing to think that I missed all the cow pats and molehills that littered those West Country fields.

My father gave up the chase after only 30 minutes. I think he figured she would come home soon enough. For me, it was a matter of life and death; I had to find her before some dog did. Eventually, in response to my calls, Rusty came whimpering up to my legs. She was wet all over her back and I knew I was too late. I held her close to me and cried. I felt that I had betrayed her and needed to find a way to hide her from my father. On the way back home I could hear him calling my name.

When we caught up to him, he grabbed me by the shoulders and told me firmly never to do that again. He had been worried for my safety and this concern was stronger than his threat to shoot Rusty if she got pregnant. I could breathe again; she was safe, this time, anyway.

•

Having failed the "eleven plus" exam, the first secondary school I went to was an all-girls one that placed a heavy emphasis on academic achievement and sport.

I was interested in neither of these subjects at the time and I did poorly at both. I no longer wore a calliper on my left leg for support but I still walked with the aid of a walking stick. My coordination was poor and so was my judgement, especially when it came to jumping over the "horse" in the gym.

I tried all sorts of routines to avoid this, but to no avail. The teacher assumed I was lazy and only pushed me harder. Allowances were made for my leg's weakness, but unfortunately this only fuelled the belief that I needed to exercise! Needless to say, I often hurt myself because I could not function properly.

Eventually, due to the hospital's insistence on hydrotherapy, it became apparent that I had a real gift for swimming. As a younger child I had found it difficult and it took me several months to grasp it. At the age of nine, however, it happened. I finally learned the art of how to float and propel myself without sinking. I can remember my excitement and jubilation and I swam at every opportunity, in all sorts of weather.

When my physical education teacher realised I was good at swimming and enjoyed the activity, she began to take more notice of me.

She entered me in lots of competitions and I won several trophies. This was all fine and I did enjoy swimming but after a while the pressure of performing began to have a negative effect on me. The fear of success and what that might mean began to dawn on me: would I be expected to make speeches or travel to faraway places? They might make me do things I could not do.

This fear was so strong that I started to deliberately lose in some of the events. I would develop cramp or complain that my leg was painful and I could not continue the swim. At other times I just slowed down and came second, instead of first. This worked for me and I successfully aborted any opportunity I might have had to develop a career in that area.

Secondary school life posed many problems for me because I could not keep up with the work and was considered lazy, slow and immature for my age. I would get class timetables and rooms muddled and was often unprepared for lessons. Homework was usually forgotten or badly done. School was a confusing place to be and I dreaded having to go.

Fortunately for me, my family moved often and I did not have to stay at any one school for very long. I say fortunately because the moves helped me "save face". Each new school gave me a fresh start and an opportunity to try again; it was also assumed that I could work as well as the next person and my academic history never followed me.

Of course today I know that the lack of continuity was not helpful to me, and indeed handicapped my progress even more.

Between the ages of 11 and 17, I attended five different secondary schools. The last one was in Frome, Somerset, and holds my happiest and saddest school memories. My English teacher there thought I had potential and commented "Excellent work, far above the standard for this class" on one of my essays. I will never forget that teacher because he inspired and helped me to believe I could achieve good work.

In post-war England, right up until the 1980s, school lunches were the norm. Children did not bring their own to school or go home to eat. Everyone ate a cooked meal provided by the school canteen at a weekly cost of five shillings per child.

At most of the schools I attended this was not a problem. We ate fish on Fridays, shepherd's pie on Mondays and

55

chicken pie or meat pie on Wednesdays. Dessert was usually rice pudding and prunes, semolina pudding and strawberry syrup, apple pie and custard, spotted dick and custard, or bread and butter pudding with custard. I always knew what to expect and always sat at the same table.

But when I was 13 years old, I attended a school that was more modern and progressive in its outlook. It offered menus and food from other countries – I felt miserable and completely lost! For the whole six months I attended that school, I rarely ate lunch.

To make a decision about what to eat for lunch was too difficult and I was afraid of attempting new tastes that looked, smelt and *were* different. Maybe this could have been remedied if it had been built into my routine that new foods were part of some meals.

Apart from this, school was fraught with other problems. The biggest difficulty was relating to the other students.

They soon tired of my repetitive stories and apparent lack of sensitivity towards their needs. Throughout my school life I was spat at, kicked, mocked and terrorised, and when I was teased or laughed at, it seemed best to pretend not to notice. I was totally unaware of the effect I had on other people or of their responses towards me. Intimacy and genuine care frightened me because I could not understand what they meant.

"Ha, ha, ha!" Laughter came from children in the row behind me during assembly, which had just begun. The headmistress was asking us to be seated.

"Ow!" I said, rather loudly. Faces turned to stare and more children giggled. Hymnbooks had been awkwardly placed on my chair so I couldn't sit down, and the boy behind me pulled my hair. I pushed the books off my chair; the noise they made as they hit the floor echoed across the school hall and the boys behind me gave a strange look. I think they meant to intimidate me — and they were successful. It was not so much that I was afraid of the other children, but I never knew what to expect next and this made me very insecure.

Being different, in whatever way, seems to upset other people. It can make them nervous, angry, abusive and indifferent, and these reactions to me were always strong. I thought everyone saw the world in the way I did, and it was very confusing for me when my delights and ecstasies were not seen or understood by other people.

At that time, being alone did not really bother me — I was happy with my own company. One thing that did disturb me was how other people seemed to enjoy each other's company and actively sought friendships and relationships. I was often asked by my aunts whether I had a boyfriend. My answer was always "yes" because there were two boys who played football with me at the farm, and they were my friends.

There were certain people whose company I did want, but unfortunately my ambivalence when I was close to them caused discomfort for all concerned. Recognition and acceptance were very important but the knowledge of how to make friends escaped me. My emotions did draw me to some of the girls in school, perhaps because of a low, gentle voice, or ability to please a teacher.

I was fixated with Connie, a girl in my form at school. She would play the piano during lunch times and allow me to sit and listen. The music, calming and repetitive, held my attention.

One of the tunes Connie played was The Seekers' *Morningtown Ride*.

"Train whistle blowing ... out along the bay ... all the little travellers are warm and snug inside..." I could actually imagine the children under their blankets with the wind blowing and the rain pouring.

I thought that Connie was beautiful and so clever to be able to play the piano. I followed her everywhere, and it was difficult to understand why she wanted me to go away at times, or why she wanted to be with other children, and not me. Now I understand that I was too needy, that my constant presence was uncomfortable for her and I demanded too much.

It is with sadness that I remember my childhood school days. I know that I lived with constant fear and confusion but it never occurred to me to ask for help or understanding. Apparently it never occurred to anyone else either!

I left school at the age of 15 and attempted to continue my education at Taunton Technical College in the west of England. At that time, I was eager to prove to the world that I was as capable as the next 15 year old.

•

A Point to Ponder

I find it quite amazing today that a child like me could be exposed to 10 years of formal education without any teacher realising or recommending special help or assistance. It appears that during my growing years children were either dumb or clever, good or bad!

I have often wondered why my parents did not appear to notice that I was different from other children. Actually I think that they did notice, but, for reasons I will never know, chose to ignore that difference. Maybe it was all too difficult at the time, or they were just too busy. Maybe they thought I was just clumsier and less mature than most other children and would grow out of it.

Chapter 7

Where To After School?

After spending so much time in hospital during my adolescence, I was familiar and comfortable with the routine and decided I wanted to become a nurse. Over the next two years I studied five O level units, as they were called, for my General Certificate of Education as a Pre-student Nurse.

I was able to pass the English language unit during my first year, so I was allowed to study (Royal Society of Arts) English with a literature unit at the advanced level. I studied this unit in my second year with three other pre-nursing students – and to my utter delight, I was the only one to pass it!

I loved studying and did well at it. Words and books began to translate into meaning and would hold my attention for hours. My emotions, however, were still out of reach and the daily demands of living away from home were very difficult.

The first boarding house I stayed in had separate quarters. The landlord was a prison officer and very strict about schedules, such as meals and night-time curfew. It was policy that I had to be in my room by nine o'clock each evening. The routine was terrific – I always knew what to expect. I was very vulnerable, however, and because I took people at their word, I believed any thing that was told to me.

One evening I made plans to attend a meeting with Alan, a Salvation Army officer who had been kind to me and always had time to talk. I explained that I had to be home by nine o'clock.

"Oh, that's fine. The meeting should end at 7.30pm."

"Is it a special meeting – I mean, why are you asking me to come?"

"Actually, I'm going to a different church tonight," he answered. "My curiosity has been aroused by a friend who goes often. He says people get healed at these meetings and delivered from evil spirits."

The church was packed. There were even people sitting on the floor along the aisles. Derrick Prince, apparently well known for his faith and ministry, was the pastor and preacher on this occasion. People clapped, sang, danced and appeared to do very much what they wanted. To my eyes and understanding at that time, it seemed the world had gone quite mad! The noise and confusion caused me to feel totally lost and bewildered.

I sat throughout the meeting, too scared to move, unable to think or understand what was happening. What made matters worse was that it was after midnight before Alan got me home.

"Wendy, I'll speak with you in the morning," my landlord said loudly, dressed only in his underpants and vest as he opened the door. I knew I was in for trouble!

I moved into my next accommodation a short time later. I was sure this would be a much more understanding place to live. The lady of the house owned over 40 dogs, several of which lived in the house with us.

"Wendy, to be quite honest with you, I'm moving away because I can't stand the way you smell," said my friend, Jane.

What did she mean? I thought I smelt just like any one else – with my nose.

Jane was a good friend, and continued.

"Wendy, do you use deodorant?" I did not know what deodorant was, so I could not say whether I used it or not. Whether it was my vacant expression or just the fact that I had not answered her, but Jane explained that I had an unpleasant odour about me. Maybe after I showered in the mornings, she suggested, I needed to use a stronger deodorant.

As far as I knew there wasn't a shower at Mrs Green's house, and no hot water either. I never showered in the mornings – in fact, the only time I used water to wash was when it was time for a meal. Mum had told me that I should always wash my hands before a meal, so I did.

"Do you shower every morning and use a strong deodorant?" I inquired.

"Well I find my roll-on is fine and it has a nice fragrance too. Boots sell it. We can go there after school if you like."

Jane and I were often together at college. I thought she was wonderful. Jane had been to boarding school and it was very difficult for the other students to see past her "posh" accent and cultured upbringing. To me, we shared a sense of "difference" and I knew that deep down inside Jane was hurting very much. I could not understand what was happening for her but she made me feel safe, warm and alive. Maybe it was the fact that I understood what it was like to be misunderstood, afraid and confused?

I became Jane's shadow, and this disturbed her very much.

"That Wendy person, I can't stand her. I wish she would leave me alone." The words stung deeply and I did not understand why she would write such words in her diary. I could not ask her about them because I felt really bad that I had read her diary. I remember later walking across the moors with Jane and her little Yorkshire terrier. The moors were really misty and the air seemed to cling to the silence that surrounded us. Neither of us spoke and although my heart ached, I felt the pain was worth it, just to be in her presence.

In many ways, Jane was my saviour. I thought she was an angel. I loved the way the sunlight danced upon her chestnut red hair and her middle class family background intrigued me. More than anything else, I wanted for us to be friends.

It was some time later that we actually talked and Jane confessed she had felt I was really weird, but "when someone gets to know you, you are okay."

Although we went our separate ways when college was over, we have kept in contact. Whatever it is that Jane touched in my life, it was good! It brought me life and inspiration and enabled me to "feel" in so many ways.

"'Leaf' it alone," she laughed, as my shoes scuffed swiftly through the old autumn leaves covering the park grass.

"You should 'branch' out," I laughed, as my hands clipped the over hanging branches of the large oaks that lined our walkway. Then, making a last running effort, we threw ourselves down to rest on the soft downy grass that covered the clearing.

The sun was warm on our bodies and the dappled shade of the nearby trees flickered across our faces as we laughed together. It was so good to laugh and to feel accepted in the company of another.

My teenage years were full of wanderings and walkabouts. Friends like Jane were very rare. For most of the time, when I was not at school or studying, I walked with my dog or attended church meetings where I felt welcome.

Looking back, I think I wanted to be like Lesley, the nurse who had made such an impression upon me at Frenchay Hospital, and this was another reason for choosing Taunton Technical College and the pre-nursing course. I thoroughly enjoyed the study, but learning the social skills of interrelating with other teenagers was almost beyond me. It was so hard to understand what they required of me; just being around others was often too much.

•

At 17, I found myself at the end of my course and it was time for more change. I needed to return home to wait for replies to my applications for student nurse training.

It was then I noticed that the problems between my parents had become intolerable. Six months later, Dad left home. Home had always been changing, with more than 12 moves before I was 17 years old, and nine different schools.

"Dad, are you leaving because of me?"

"Oh no, Wendy, and you must never blame yourself for what has happened between your mother and I." Dad's voice sounded different – a bit like it sounded before he went to bed. I concluded he must have been tired. In spite of his words, my feeling of somehow being responsible for my parent's separation did not leave me.

Over the past 30 years or so I have concluded that with most of the events I encountered – I felt personally responsible in some way or other. This may be true for other Asperger people; it corresponds with the black and white perspective we seem to have.

I tried to think about my future. Nursing was my goal and so I chose to enrol as a student nurse at the Guildford school of Nursing in Surrey, England. I lived in the nurses' home and visited my mother or father every now and then. I felt like a stranger at such times; communication between us was difficult. I could not explain my world to my family and I could not function fully in theirs.

Chapter 8

Farewell To Childhood

I was still in my teens when my parent's divorce came through. Mum managed a bottle shop in Guildford but on many occasions the bottle managed her! I think this was her way of coping with her grief over my father's perceived betrayal of their relationship. Her behaviour isolated me even more. I did not understand her, and felt angry that she was not in control when I needed her to be.

In spite of the family discord, for the first few months I seemed to succeed with the demands of the student-nursing course. Then responsibility loomed. My success had been in my ability to enter into the routine of ward life – this was something I could do well. Of course, this didn't last – decisions were required to be made and I was required to make them! I found myself forgetting the instructions I was given, or getting them confused. I still didn't sleep well at night and in the darkness lived all sorts of monsters.

I was afraid: afraid to be around people; afraid of not being able to keep up the performance. I crashed!

This was a very black time. I don't recall the events leading up to my admission to the institution. I only remember that my head seemed disconnected from my body and I felt desperate to get it back. Everywhere I went, shadows seemed to follow me. Dark, hooded figures offered to relieve me of my life and disconnect me from the pain. The psychiatrist referred to these shadows as "voices". I knew I had to outrun them – to give in to them would have been too easy.

I could not trust them and I could not take the risk of allowing them to get too close. The doctors saw my agitation and constant mobility as undesirable and prescribed Largactil to calm me down. After being on this drug for many months, I knew the shadows had won. My very lifeblood felt sucked dry and I had no desire to relate to anyone or anything.

Prior to leaving college, I had met a young man on one of the visits to my parent's home. During the college Christmas break, I attended the service at a local church in the village. After the service the young people were going to a Folkstone church for a special "get together".

Tony, 18 at the time, offered me a lift on his matchless 500cc motorbike. He had kind eyes but I could tell that social interaction was painful for him. This mutual understanding and a desire to help in some way were the basis for beginning a friendship. I wanted to enter his world and make it less lonely. In Tony's presence, I tried to be normal, to do what was expected of me and even cultivate a girlfriend-boyfriend type relationship.

We did not spend lots of time together because Tony lived in Kent and I was studying in Somerset. At one point in the relationship, I needed to explain to him that I was not physically attracted to him, and found intimacy and affection very difficult. He said this was not a problem to him. On reflection, I think affection was also difficult for him and without too much intimacy the relationship was less complicated.

Tony was born in the house he lived in. He had never moved and although he had few friends, there was something stable about him. I think my perceived sense of his stability was based on my limited knowledge of his upbringing. He was one of eight children, and his grandparents, aunts, uncles and cousins all lived locally. My family was widespread throughout the west and south east of England, and contact with extended family members was limited.

Tony was a man of few words, but his commitment to keeping the church clean and getting the fire going to warm the building impressed me. He seldom complained, gossiped or criticised other people. Here is a man who can be gentle and undemanding, I thought.

We could not communicate in any depth, but it seemed enough to be in each other's company, and so the relationship continued. Both Tony and I were very naive and unprepared for an adult relationship. (I say this on reflection because it is only now, after 20 years of married life and four years of divorce, that I am beginning to understand what an adult communicative relationship actually means!)

Although we shared little in a deep and meaningful way, Tony appeared to be loyal and committed to our relationship. His letters to me always said the same thing: "Dear Wendy, how are you? I am fine ... from Tony." Reading or writing was a trial for him and so his letters held just enough to say he was thinking about me and he was well.

Over time, I became irritated with his lack of ability to make decisions and apparent poor communication skills. However, I decided that his other qualities – loyalty and commitment – were more important, so I tried to overlook the things that upset me.

After some time, probably three years, of communicating from a distance, Tony made the break from his home village and family. He moved into my mother's house in Guildford, Surrey. We had separate bedrooms but it was assumed we would marry and find a place of our own. I was 19 years old and training to become a State Registered Nurse.

Sharing the house with us were my mother, sister and two of my church friends — a brother and sister. Maggie was a year older than me, an art student who played guitar and enchanted me with her musical and artistic abilities.

"Here Wendy, you can colour in these Christmas cards I've drawn, then we can send them out." I felt so honoured and spent hours colouring the cards with accurate precision, never messing up the colours or going over the lines. Just to think that Maggie would trust me to carry out such a task made me love her even more!

Tony rarely held my attention like Maggie and when offered a choice between time with her or time with Tony, I chose Maggie every time. She was an obsession, an absolute compulsion and I delighted in her company. She and I had been living in Mum's house for two years; we were as inseparable as a body and its shadow at noon.

Then one summer's morning, she announced she was leaving, going west to find work.

"Oh Wendy, darling, you are going to marry Tony and I think it's time to move on. It's okay, little one, we'll always be friends, and I will always be with you."

I just could not believe what she was saying. I had never considered I would have to face life without her. Who would sing our songs? Who would colour in her pictures? Who would call me "little one" when I was upset?

Just over a month after Maggie left, I married Tony. The wedding was simple. I decorated the hall with wild flowers from the country lanes near my mother's home — pink ragged robins, buttercups, celandines, white daisies, pink and white clover, long green grasses and some white cow parsley flowers. In my bouquet I carried white freesias and lily-of-the-valley. These were two of my favourite flowers and I adored their fragrances.

A thankful patient's wife made my dress. A simple, high waisted white frock with a velvet ribbon running just under the breast line. An older woman from church made the two-tier wedding cake. We stood the cake on an old red record player covered with a white broderie anglaise cloth. Preparing for our wedding was not difficult and did not cost heaps of money, as friends brought buffet-type foods and both the dress and cake were gifts.

A big coach brought my relatives from Somerset and Tony's family came by car, from Kent. During the signing of the register, two friends from the hospital sang a duet and then one of them told a story of loss and hope.

It was so easy to get caught up in all of the preparations for the wedding and lose the reality of how to prepare for a marriage ... I loved the flower decorations in the church hall and felt a real connection with the colourful festivities. Connection to Tony however, and the reality of a lifelong committed relationship — with all that entailed — was far from me.

I missed Maggie beyond belief but made my wedding vows with utter sincerity before the Church, congregation and God. That day was one of the loneliest I can remember. I went to the hairdresser on my own and she styled my hair with lots of pins and hair lacquer. I hated the procedure. In the past I had only been to a hairdresser on a few occasions because usually I cut my own hair. I struggled with wearing the wedding gown and the veil, telling myself that I could put my other clothes back on later.

This all took place on the 6th of May, 1972. It was Cup Final day and I was oblivious to the fact that my relatives were anxious to return home and watch the match on telly. My father did not come to the wedding because of the rift with Mum. He also had a new wife, whom I liked very much, and this complicated things for all the family. It was hard for me to understand all of this and I felt that he should have been there. I missed having him to "give me away", a job my brother took on. These were the facts however, and I chose to accept them.

For a wedding present, two good friends paid for Tony and I to stay for two nights in the bridal suite at a Clevedon hotel in the west of England. Neither of us were familiar with hotel etiquette and we both felt rather uncomfortable.

After our arrival, we were shown to our room. We hadn't eaten much at the reception and Tony was hungry. He asked for some toast and milk and followed the porter to get it. On his return, he tripped over the red hall carpet, spilling the milk everywhere! Poor Tony, he looked so helpless but I just wished he was more assertive and not so clumsy.

It was getting late and we were both very tired. I spent over an hour trying to comb out the pins and lacquer from the hairdresser; I later learnt that they were supposed to stay in and that the "hairdo" was meant to last for a while!

The room had a lovely view over the sea and within a short time we were both asleep. The next morning we awoke to breakfast in bed – a wonderful English breakfast of eggs, bacon, toast, tea and marmalade. I felt uncomfortable about being given breakfast while I was still in bed, but coped with that.

I do not remember what we did that day but I do remember returning rather late to the hotel and that we had been locked out! Fortunately Tony found a side fire escape door unlocked and that lead onto the balcony where he was able to open the window of the room where we were staying. I enjoyed the feeling of climbing into the room through the window and thought we were having quite an adventure.

When we returned to my mother's home after our honeymoon, my life began to feel very depressing. For the next two years, I drifted in and out of depression and was unmotivated towards anything.

My nursing career had ceased. Because I had been afraid and confused, I had never finished my student nurse training. I found the ward routine rewarding but the integration of new working principles and changing methods of operations was too taxing for me at the time. I often forgot procedures, especially if they were not routine and mundane. I was so afraid of getting it wrong that I needed to go off duty on sick leave rather than attempt the task.

There is one time I remember very well. I was 17 and waiting to start my training at Guildford. For a few months I worked as a cadet nurse and loved it so much. After just a few weeks, I asked if I could work on night duty. The very adventure of the idea thrilled me — however, I was not able to think ahead and anticipate the responsibility such a venture would require.

My request was granted and I was given the solo responsibility of the children's ward at night. Most of the patients were routine T's and A's (tonsils and adenoids) which meant that post-operatively I took their pulse, respiration and temperature every 15 minutes. This was done to check the child was recovering well and not bleeding from their wound.

I also set up breakfast trays and re-packed the sterilisers, as well as seeing to any of the children's toiletry needs — I was in my element. During the night I heated up any leftovers from the children's supper in the steriliser, along with the metal kidney bowls, and enjoyed a meal during my dinner break.

Night duty during my student nurse days, however, was more demanding. One night, the women's medical ward was short staffed and I was sent to help out. When I arrived I was shown into a side ward where a middle-aged woman lay dead of cancer. The senior night nurse then left me with the words, "start washing her, I'll be back when I have finished the drugs."

I was unmoved by the fact that this was my first "dead person" and I could not understand the Night Sister's concern when she heard I had been left alone with this lady. To add to the tone of the night, it was very wet and stormy outside, with the winds whistling through the corridors and wards. I was unaware of all these emotions and fear connections, and while the other nurses found this strange, I found it to be an asset.

After about two years working as a nurse at the Guildford Hospital, I could not hide my inability to cope with either change or complicated procedures any more. It was time to face the reality that I was not able to continue. There were many incidents that seem laughable to me now (and indeed, some were at the time) and I'm sure my guardian angel protected both me and the patients in my care.

"Nurse, where are Mr. Watson's false teeth?"

Mr. Watson had required a blanket bath after a small accident with his bowels. It was almost bedtime, so it seemed like a good idea to take out his false teeth and settle him down for the night. Unfortunately, Sister called me into her office for the changeover report that needed to be given to the night nurses coming on duty. I had put Mr Watson's teeth into my pocket, intending to wash them and put them into his tooth mug after Sister had finished her report.

My intentions were swallowed up by the fact that after report it was time to go off duty. It was at 7.30 the next morning that I received the phone call asking me where his teeth were. How could I explain myself? It made perfect sense to me to do what I had done — unfortunately, the Duty Sister did not see it that way.

Leaving the nursing profession was indeed traumatic and I often went back to the wards for visits. These visits put me in touch with a feeling of "belonging" and I felt so much at home.

At the age of 20 I attempted suicide, feeling no reason to continue with life. My source of life had gone. Maggie had decided I was strange and had demons inside me. She did not stay in contact and when our paths crossed at a later date she would not acknowledge my presence. Her behaviour was too difficult for me to understand and her rejection of me too hard to cope with.

Due to my apparent apathy towards life and my desperate depression, I was admitted into a mental institution for observation. My memories of that time are scarce but the bits I do recall are vivid. I remember the large moths that flew high up on the ceilings of the huge open wards.

"Don't worry, love, they are only man-eating moths," another patient said, giggling at my apparent dread of these fluttering creatures. Oh, it's good that I am a woman then, I thought.

A deep dark awareness of depression and nothingness overtook me. I was terrified. My marriage to Tony felt so dead and my efforts to relate to him sexually, emotionally or even as a friend seemed empty and unrewarding. I could not conjure up any emotion, even though I really wanted to please him.

He had his own problems ... maybe he realised he could not reach me, or maybe it was his own impotence and lack of communication skills, but life was very difficult for both of us. There were times when only the routine of the hospital ward kept me on track.

Unfortunately, I did not know then how to find help or even what kind of help to look for. After 14 months of marriage, I entered the institution for the second time. I was considered to be having "another schizophrenic episode". Completely withdrawn and feeling I had fallen into a bottomless pit, I was placed on a program of medication.

The ward life continued around me, and without me. Sucking the roof of my mouth and rocking myself kept me sane. Two months later I was told I was pregnant, and all medication ceased. The corridors in my head kept leading me into larger and larger rooms and the walls of these rooms were hard and unforgiving. When I knocked my head against these walls, nothing changed. I could not stop the sense of emptiness creeping over me and only the softness of the daisies in the hospital garden gave me a sense of peace.

At least the meals were regular and I got excited at the different colours on the dinner plate. The orange of the carrots against the roundness of the green peas and the white fluffy potatoes covered in brown gravy made me smile. I loved the colours and I loved meal times. They kept me linked to life and I counted the hours between lunch and teatime.

The ward where I slept was very depressing. Patients were forbidden to sleep there during the day, but this was often the time when I felt most sleepy. Electric Convulsive Therapy (ECT) was discussed, but fortunately it was never tried on me.

"Don't let them fry your brain, Wendy," Angie in the next bed said. "My memory ain't been the same since they gave me 'the treatment'. They just want you to become vegetables, that's all — vegetables!"

Eventually I was released from Brookwood Hospital and on the journey home in a neighbour's car, my head said, "Never again, never again will this happen to me. If they think I am mad, then I must prove them wrong."

•

A Point to Ponder

It was 25 years before that diagnosis was overturned. I was diagnosed with Asperger's syndrome after spending time with a psychologist at a well-known Melbourne University in August 1994. It was a relief to be told I was not schizophrenic — but also scary to realise I had some other ailment that had no cure. Asperger's syndrome was not translated into the English language until 1991, although Mr Asperger recorded it as a condition related to autism in 1943!

Chapter 9

Children Of My Own

When I was released from the institution, I was already three months pregnant. This realisation was difficult to comprehend and the thought of another life forming within me was just amazing. The possibility of motherhood had not occurred to me, especially as I had not experienced full intercourse with Tony. Apparently I had conceived anyway! To celebrate my pregnancy, I walked into the village and bought a baby's bib from the general store.

I hadn't had morning sickness or any other signs, but somehow the bib made things more tangible. I thought about preparing for my baby and decided to paint murals on a few of the walls in our flat. I chose my favourite colours: greens, purple and blue.

I painted an emerald green boat on a pastel green sea. The boat had purple oars and deep blue fish swam in the sea. In one corner of the pale green sky, a bright spider-like sun shone down, casting its light upon the fish. This picture completely occupied the landing wall, and was the first thing seen upon entry to our flat.

On the opposite dining room wall, just around the corner, I painted the story of creation. This began with a tiny spider in a web on one corner of the wall and spread out to the tall mountains of the opposite corner. In the middle were two stick-like characters, representing the human race, and all around them were hills, valleys, trees, stars, the sun and the moon. Poppy-like flowers splattered red and yellow shadows at 90° angles with various green stems and leaves. A purple dog barked and two seagulls flew overhead. I wanted my baby to have a full and colourful introduction to his new home.

I made mobiles from silver and gold milk bottle tops, pink and green egg boxes, and blobs of white cotton wool – these all hung at various levels on long pieces of black cotton thread from a metal coat hanger. A good friend gave me a wooden cot, painted mauve, and other bits of paraphernalia. Her own baby had never used them.

So there I was, nine months later, ready (if that's possible) for my first baby. The pregnancy had gone well and I had kept mostly to myself, at home, being maternally minded. I was, however, unsure of what to expect next. At the relaxation classes they told us to breathe in a certain way and stay in control. They said that gas and air could be offered to help us cope with any contractions that were very uncomfortable, and injections of pethidine could be given for greater discomfort. The word "pain" was not used and the midwife said our worst enemy was fear. Well, I was terrified and dreaded going into labour!

One of the friends I made while I was nursing worked in the labour ward. I prayed she would be present, but I was one week overdue. A decision was made to induce labour. On reflection, I think this was just convenient for the doctors!

At 9.30am my waters were broken in one of the most painful experiences I had ever had. By four o'clock the next morning, I was in a lot of pain. The contractions were regular and utterly unbearable; I thought I was going to die.

I couldn't cope with gas and air because with a mask over my face I felt like I was suffocating. I asked for an alterative to pethidine because this drug made me vomit. The doctor said he would give me some feldine – not as effective as pethidine, but with less side effects.

The injection made me really sick. Vomiting and striving so hard to stay with it, I felt betrayed, knowing I had not been believed and had been given pethidine after all. It was as if Tony and the medical staff were conspiring against me, laughing at my predicament. The midwife told me that having a baby was so natural, it couldn't be as bad as I was making it out to be. Thousands of babies were born every day – she told me to stop making such a fuss. I felt myself withdrawing and I gave into the pain ... now was as good a time as any to die. I felt very much alone.

My baby son was born at 6am, but by this time I was closed off. I needed several stitches, and then I was taken back to the ward. They said the baby was fine, although he was a bit jaundiced and very sleepy. He had received my pethidine too. I didn't see him for 24 hours.

After the delivery, I withdrew. I curled up into a ball and tried to comfort myself by sucking the roof of my mouth. The nursing staff left me alone and I slept on until the early hours of the next morning. When I awoke, I remembered I had a baby and I knew I needed to act like a mother or else I might lose him. I wanted very much to be able to care for my son and I felt determined that I would do so. I went on to automatic pilot, trying to copy the other mums.

Breast-feeding was very painful and it took over a week to learn the art. One of the midwives sat on the bed, took my nipple and placed it into my son's puckered mouth, and expected him to be able to feed. Not only was this extremely uncomfortable but it also stressed him.

I longed to be left alone, to go home and have uninterrupted time with my son. I just wanted to adapt and to get to know this new little person. Tony was so happy to have a son, but it did not occur to him to buy me flowers or his son a teddy bear. I noticed the other new mums had these things and I felt a pang of jealousy. I did not understand then that Tony was a lot like me and it was very hard for him to know what I wanted from him.

We left the hospital ten days after the delivery. The baby was a gem. He slept a lot and I didn't feel afraid of him — my only fear was that I would misread him in some way and not be able to meet all his needs. In spite of my fears, we made a very good team and I soon learned what he needed and how to respond to him.

•

MIRACLE

Baby, baby sleeping sound, where is it that you go?
To the forest, underground to the sea or snow?
You seem to lie so still and quiet;
can I share your dreams?
I will love and care for you, whatever that may mean.
When you feel sad or very glad, I want to hear your voice.
Communication may be tough but it will be our choice.

•

After a few months, the doctors decided I was suffering from post-natal depression and needed medication again. I knew I was functioning well but was detached from the whole affair ... so what was new? My whole life, I had lived with a sense of being estranged. The only place I felt truly safe and at home was inside myself.

My world was separate from *the* world and could be accessed simply. I could suck the roof of my mouth, run my fingers over some soft material, fix upon some twinkling colours or lights – and I would be home. It took great effort to resist the temptation to retreat and run home. At times I just had to get out of the house – walk across the fields or down the country lanes – and I would put my son on my back and we would go off for our adventures together. During such times, no one could invade my space or ask me to make decisions about things. I could just be.

The doctors however were concerned and felt I needed therapy, so I went back as a day patient. During these times, my son stayed in the creche. I still fed him and cared for his needs, but I often felt a panic attack coming over me when it neared time for his meals. It was vital to me I was not late and there for my son when he woke up, or wanted me. I did not want him to feel abandoned.

On a Tuesday evening, once a week, Tony came to the sessions. The idea was that we would get in touch with our emotions, but the whole idea terrified me and I could feel a big black nothingness coming up from the pit of my stomach. The thought of not being able to be normal, of having my baby taken away from me and losing all that I had fought to find, motivated me to keep attending therapy. We were told to join hands with the person next to us and walk around in a circle. The emotions I experienced made me feel sick, not connected and secure, as intended.

I did find a friend in this group though, and she seemed to accept me for who I was. When the sessions stopped, I would go to her house, once a week or so, where I could watch and learn as she interacted with her two children.

My son hated being cuddled and only slept in his cot. This was a problem if Tony and I were visiting friends or relations some distance from home, and our son needed to sleep on the way. To stop him crying, we had to stop the car, physically remove him from his car seat, spank him on his hand and then sit with him in the back seat, restraining him until he tired of fighting and gave in to sleep. I hated this routine and went out as little as possible. As long as his home routine was maintained, my son was content, but if I so much as rearranged his bedroom furniture, he would become very upset and refuse to sleep.

Friends of ours who had children thought James' behaviour was bizarre and his world should revolve around us, not the other way around. Their lack of routine made me anxious however, as I fully understood how important routine was for James.

It was never difficult to hold James, but it had to be on his terms. If he was afraid or hurt. I always had the feeling we were not really communicating — not in any depth, but on the superficial level of routine living. Other mothers seemed to delight in touching their children and would ask them to come up and have a cuddle, or give them a kiss. I only wanted to be there for my son, be available to him. It worried me that we did not seem to need to cuddle and kiss each other all the time.

When James was a year old, my daily visits to the institution stopped. I was told to stay on the medication, an injection given to me monthly by my general practitioner. Check-up appointments every six months were made with the psychiatrist, and a social worker, Julie, visited me regularly. The district nurse came to see the baby.

Tony tried to relate to his son but James felt insecure with him. I tried to relate to Tony too, but it was always at a distance; neither of us was able to meet the needs of the other. We compromised and a routine of what was required from us became the ritual, enabling us to cope with everyday life. I ached inside and longed for it to be different, but it never was.

Over the next eight years, I had three more children. My last was born just after my 30th birthday. Family life was very full and the children were on the go from 6am until late at night. I did not have much time to think about myself, and just operated on automatic pilot most of the time.

On reflection, I think I felt very empty but I could not work out what my feelings were. On the one hand, I wanted to have friends, but on the other I feared being rejected by people. It was much safer to keep my distance, maintain a routine for my family life and retreat into my own world when life presented problems for which I had no answer.

"Would you be interested in a lift to playschool? I have to take my children there twice a week, and we could go together," asked Pat. Her words brought a sense of both relief and panic. I was grateful for the offer of transport because it was a five mile walk or bike ride. The playschool was in the next village. I didn't want James and Mary to miss out just because of the distance.

Pat and I shared the playschool run and also stayed at the hall with our children. She seemed keen to be a friend and often talked about things that were problems for her. I did my best to listen, especially when she shared her concern over feeling depressed and unmotivated. As I understood from my doctor that I also had these problems, it became a talking point for us.

Pat lived in a flat above me and so her children kept company with mine on a daily basis. I was babysitter for them on many occasions because she came from South Africa and found the chores of being a housewife very hard. In South Africa, they always had a houseboy and girl who took care of these things, including childcare.

I spent lots of time with the children. It was a very safe place to be. It did not matter whether I played games with them on the floor, did finger-painting, played with home-made playdough or joined in hide-and-seek, they never said I was dumb or stupid!

As the children grew older, my involvement with the local mothers' groups I had been invited to attend increased. I usually played with the children or took care of them while the other mothers talked. I did not feel safe in adult company and was afraid I would be asked questions I could not answer. I did attend some of their functions but always busied myself by offering to wash the dishes or clear up in some way. This covered my fear of interaction and intimacy.

I even managed to acquire two cleaning jobs with a couple of the mums. They thought I was very good and allowed me to babysit for them when they went out. I felt both proud and privileged being asked to do this and always made sure that I had relevant contact telephone numbers in case of an emergency.

Chapter 10

The Middle Years

As my children grew older it became more difficult to cover up my sense of inadequacy. Tony started his own business and was working long and unfriendly hours. There were times when he did not have any work or was not paid for the job he had done – difficult, because we did not have any alternative finance. I relied on the goodwill of others to help us in such circumstances, and even took food that had been put aside from our neighbour's kitchen for the animals.

The pressure of trying to make the house-keeping money cover all the domestic bills was great and I was just not able to do it. My feelings of inadequacy kept growing and the depression caused me to regress. I could feel my head splitting from my body and felt I was losing control. To help keep myself sane, I spent a lot of time in other people's homes or in the company of near neighbours. This was not because I needed their company, but to stop myself retreating. I soon began to have flashbacks from my childhood however, and could feel myself withdrawing into a world of fantasy that was much less threatening than the one in which I was living.

When I was 20 I had attempted to jump from a second storey window onto a very busy main street. Tony had been the one to find and prevent me from succeeding. Those same feelings of emptiness and despair haunted me again. I tried to talk to a couple of close friends from the church but found little understanding. How could I expect that they would comprehend what I did not understand?

The situation became very bleak. Once again I moved into detached and compulsive behaviour, but now on a more severe level than usual. I walked with my eyes directed at the ground at all times, and became obsessed with the gravel. My heightened senses noticed every pebble and every bug that was there.

I told myself that for the children's sake I needed to stay with it and not withdraw, and I always managed to do and be what they needed. However, the more I needed Tony to be strong and in control, the more he withdrew.

I believe he resented me for being needy, and felt cheated and utterly disappointed both with his own performance as a man and husband, and with mine as a wife and woman. His abusive behaviour increased and he refused to be involved with the family any longer. If I suggested it would be great for the children if he played with them or spent time with them, he felt nagged and undermined. I went to my counsellor who suggested I try to make Tony feel more important and special. I did try to do this, in spite of my own difficulties with relating, but he snubbed me.

On one occasion he picked up the special dinner I had cooked and threw it to the floor. His anger was usually non-verbal, as he preferred to thump a wall or stomp on the children's toys.

By this time, I had given up on my efforts to help him. I felt he did not really want to change — maybe it was not even possible. I did want to explore and understand my own behaviour though, so I began to read whatever I could find concerning schizophrenia and depression.

We had been married for 10 years and had spent most of that time living in someone else's home. It was a very big property and we had a separate wing of the house, but it was still someone else's place and we were constantly reminded that other people shared our lives. I longed for separateness, for a home of our own.

My mother had moved to Australia where my younger sister, aunt and uncle were already living. It was suggested that we join them. Mum said opportunities for young families were more apparent there and it would not be a problem for Tony to find work.

As his grandfather had lived in Australia, he had always been drawn to the country. We applied to emigrate, basing our application on the family reunion criteria.

The process was a lengthy one and during its course we travelled out to Australia, as a family, to see how we all felt about the possibility of living there. We landed in Melbourne on the 16th of February, 1983 — what became known as Ash Wednesday, a day of devastating bushfires in many parts of Victoria. I remember the ash that had settled upon my brother-in-law's car and the intense heat surrounding us, but with the excitement of the holiday and the family reunion, it was not such an issue.

The children found a family in the street nearby who invited them into their air-conditioned home. Here they were able to play table tennis and video games to their hearts' content. The gentleman of the household offered to employ Tony as a painter with his firm and this was helpful for our immigration application.

We stayed in Australia for seven weeks. It was an intense time of much frustration. Tony was distant and uncommunicative, and the more he withdrew, the more my sense of isolation increased. I could not reach him and only managed to cope with the demand of family life because the alternative was unthinkable.

Towards the end of the holiday, my middle son, David, became very ill. Eventually he was taken to Fairfield Hospital where he was treated for a Coccacci group three virus. To complicate matters, David also had whooping cough and ear infections. I stayed in the hospital with him and Tony had to mind our three other children at my sister's home in Mordialloc.

The hospital situation brought back all sorts of memories for me. I felt very much at home. It was easy to remember the nurses and how I had enjoyed helping them. I remembered the time of studying for my pre-nursing certificate at Taunton Technical College, and wondered why it was that studying was such a pleasure for me, but practical work experience had been such a disaster?

David recovered quickly, and we returned to England. There we pursued our immigration plans.

Less than one year later, we were again landing on Australian soil. My youngest child was two years old and my eldest, James, was 10.

Some people might consider being in a new country with new traditions and new friends as motivation for exploration and encouragement; it filled *me* with dread and depression. There had been a time for hope and renewed motivation, but these feelings were short-lived.

A saving grace was the kindness of our neighbours.

"Hello, I'm Carol. Would the children like these doughnuts and sandwiches? I work in a bakery and quite often we have things left over at the end of the day." Carol was a lovely lady who seemed to genuinely care, however her husband was prone to alcohol and physical abuse. He was always civil to us but I never felt comfortable in his presence. Carol could share the leftovers from her shop, but she could not share time with us. On a couple of occasions she did try, but I got the impression relating to us was difficult because of my egocentric behaviour and scruffy appearance.

Despite feeling like a fish out of water, I still possessed an enthusiasm for life that some people appeared to find uncomfortable.

Most people had their own problems and did not want to be involved with mine. Some folk at the church we attended tried to relate to us, but never really moved beyond first base.

I would attach myself to certain women in the church who seemed to be interesting or offered friendship, but it was not long before they suddenly became unavailable or disinterested in me. This was always difficult to understand. Why is it that someone can say they want to get to know you, share their lives with you, and then pull away when you disappoint them or become too demanding?

Before we had left England, Tony had promised we could return home if we were unhappy after 12 months in Australia. One year later, the children and I were still feeling very homesick and pleaded with him to take us home. He said no, and my isolation continued. I joined a Christian outreach group and buried myself in its various programs, hoping to find some relief. This was a profitable time and I discovered I had leadership abilities.

I was often asked to lead the group in prayer and worship. I knew that prayer simply meant conversation with God and worship meant singing, so I talked out loud the thoughts that were in my head and sang one of my favourite choruses. This seemed to work well; people enjoyed my prayers and my songs and said it was a nice change to be part of a time of such simplicity and spontaneity. For my personal life, though, confrontation with emotions and reality was still a long way off.

My hunger for information and understanding pursued me like a lost dog. The more I read about depression and schizophrenia, the more I was convinced these conditions did not belong to me. I certainly owned some of their symptoms, and some of my behaviour was typical, but too much of it was not.

After being in Australia for six years, my marriage had never looked shakier. I began to have dreams that Tony was chasing me with a big knife and just as it plunged into my chest I would wake up. I would wait until he was asleep at night before I went to bed, which was usually after two in the morning. We were really leading separate lives.

This living death became unbearable and I had to reach out again for counselling. Tony believed I was the problem, so he would not see the counsellor with me. I think for him to admit that he was also part of the problem was too hard, but his refusal to share the journey with me just compounded the problems and increased my feeling of isolation.

As time passed, his frustration with my inability to relate to him physically increased. His sense of self-esteem was low and his frustration took on an even more defensive mode. He would mock me and put me down, especially when we were in public.

One night in particular remains in my memory. Tony's frustration and anger caused him to vent himself upon me. This was the ultimate betrayal and the fear in our relationship intensified. In spite of almost 20 years of marriage and four children, I knew it was ending. Tony withdrew from the children and me completely. We were an intrusion and a threat, and the responsibility of providing for us was too much.

Eventually the routine we had established was not enough to maintain our everyday life. We decided to divorce.

The Christmas of 1994 was quite unlike any other in my experience. I can remember the joy and anticipation when, as a 16-year-old away from home, I sang carols in the intensive care ward of a maternity wing in a large teaching hospital. It was as if I was singing to baby Jesus himself. Those little people – so helpless and dependent, so terribly small. I thought that God took a big risk becoming a baby – but maybe that way he had a better chance to touch the stubborn, proud hearts of the human race.

This Christmas, however, carried only memories of misrepresentation and injustice. Since the divorce from Tony, my children were caught up in a battle of their own. Intellectually I understood what they were going through because I had studied the affects of divorce upon children. However, I still hoped that it would be different for my children.

After all, I loved them. It was me who had always tried to be there for them. It was me who cooked, cleaned and cared for them. And it was me who always remembered their birthdays and Christmases. I wanted them to remember me and understand my heart. How foolish of me, but I am sure many people feel this way at Christmas. I was a long way from home. To help me feel I existed and was important, I went to McDonald's for breakfast.

As always, whenever I ate breakfast there, I separated the top layer of muffin and kept it for the marmalade. I ate my sausage and cheese slice attached to one side of the muffin, then spread marmalade over the remaining half and enjoyed eating it between mouthfuls of hot coffee. This exercise offered the reassurance I lacked and afterwards I was able to resume the duties of the day.

Chapter 11

My Coming Of Age

After the divorce, I went back to school and continued with the Victorian Certificate in Education. I believe this decision really opened the door on life for me. I wanted to increase my understanding of both myself and the world around me.

Two years later, a girlfriend and I were at the local milk bar. It was 6am. We had watched the sunrise and were both eagerly awaiting the opening of the shop so we could buy the newspaper. Inside *The Age* were all the names of the successful applicants for the various universities – we were like children waiting for Santa! Our anticipation was almost painful as we scoured the columns of words for my name and ID number.

It was hard to be patient and I thought I would explode with the tension. After looking several times my friend announced that my name was not there! We sat down on the wooden seat outside the laundrette, for one last look.

My heart was pounding inside my chest and I tried to stay calm. Suddenly my friend found my name – it had been difficult to spot because the latter half of it was printed into the fold of the newspaper and it was right at the end of a column. I was jubilant. The tears rolled down my face at the relief and realisation of what it meant to have secured a place at university.

"What an achievement!" I shouted. I wanted to tell my primary school teachers who had said I was a submarine and could never surface! It was like being the first person to ever discover gold, or a genie who had the cork pulled on her bottle – now I was free! I felt the "sky was the limit" and I would fly forever. I could be anyone, go anywhere, and the world would not look down its nose at me any longer.

The possibility of obtaining a degree in social science suggested to me that I was not dumb. Why did I need to feel that way? Most of my life I had been treated as if I were not "quite right".

•

A Point To Ponder

Sometimes people spoke about me in my presence, as if I could not hear or understand what they were saying. At other times, I was treated like a child since it was assumed that was all I could understand. I have often wanted to scream and act "mad", just to fulfil the expectations of others!

Chapter 12

Learning To Cope

I have come so far in the past four years, but many aspects of day-to-day life are still very difficult for me. My brain tries so hard to "get it right". I want to relate to other people, I want to fit in somewhere, but this just does not seem to work. I often say the wrong words at the wrong time!

Relationships are still so demanding, so confusing. I want to relate to other people but I'm not sure I can survive the pain of it all. Some days my brain is so sore from trying to work out what it is I am supposed to do or to say, that I just cannot do it for very long.

There are other days when I'm working on an assignment for university and feel happy and very excited. I could write essays all day – they do not bite back at me. The written word has a form all its own. The pen between my fingers feels solid and tangible. It moves with me and allows the symbols of my pain or ecstasy to reveal themselves. Words express my distress through the pen and onto the paper and back to my mind. I can see them on the paper; they talk to me and help me to make sense of my life.

How much easier it is to hear someone if you can't see his or her face. Then words are pure and not distorted by grimaces and gestures. I can listen better to the tone of someone's voice when I am not confused by the unwritten words of their facial expressions.

I do allow myself to look into the eyes of some people. Temporarily I gain a sense of feeling lost and because I know that people look at each other when they talk, I can tell myself that the "lost" feeling will go away if I ignore it.

There are days when just trying to make sense of the rules for social interaction is too difficult. It is especially so when we take into account that individuals often write their own rules! For example, it's fine to take off your clothes to have a bath, but only a model takes off her clothes for the photographer; or you can laugh at that story, even though it's about the fat lady, because it's a joke.

•

THE WORLD IS MAD

Twiddle dee and twiddle dum
How on earth have I begun?
I started out all right you see,
But now I question who is me?

Which of these I know so well
How I wish that I could tell.
If only it could stay the same,
I'd work the rules out for this game.

They call the movie "Life" you see,
But which is them and which is me?

I know for me the words serve well
But as for others, who can tell

I thought I'd got it
But then came the shock.
You lot knew it
But I did not!

•

When I was learning to drive, my driving instructor said, "Wendy, you will have to work harder on your shoulder turns." I tried to turn my shoulder, I tried looking over my shoulder, I even tried to turn my whole body but my instructor assured me that this was not necessary. I decided that turning my head to look over my shoulder at what was behind me just was not possible for me! Once more the instructor explained to me about "the blind spot".

"You mean I don't have to look over my shoulder at all?" I said in utter disbelief. "You only want me to look towards the rear passenger window to see if anything is at the side of the car – that's the blind spot?" I felt so stupid and so angry! All of these years, at least 25 of them, I had believed I had to somehow twist my neck to see over my shoulder, to see what was directly behind me. Why had no one ever explained this to me before?

My driving instructor just looked at me. I stared out into the silence as the wind whistled past the windscreen with the passing of each car. I was not even sure I wanted to continue learning to drive – maybe I just was not meant to be a driver! Then again, they said there were many things I could not do!

No, I could not give up just yet. I would work on this business of driving a car and at least give it my best shot. After all, there had been other obstacles that seemed insurmountable but they had been knocked down to size and tackled bit by bit.

•

Autistic people find it very hard to generalise. They may learn the rules for a particular situation but will not know how to translate that into other situations.

Metaphor is the language we use to say something that carries meaning but is said in abstract terms or even in story form. I am quite good at comprehending metaphor now, except at times when the wording is unfamiliar to me. The best way to learn how to understand such talk is to ask for it to be explained to you in ordinary, logical terms, and then to rote learn the metaphor in case it should appear in conversation again.

How peaceful it is to withdraw from the complicated world of human relationships! I do however enjoy the presence of a friend and feel so content in the company of one who is willing to take me as I am. My friends have been willing to see me this way and I am so grateful to have been given the opportunities to discover life in the real world.

"Can I buy dessert now?" I asked. We were at McDonald's, my favourite eating place, and my main meal was over.

"Wendy, you don't have to ask my permission to buy dessert," my friend said. "You are an adult, you can do what you want."

But that is how it is. Due to being constantly unsure of required behaviour, I always ask my friends what needs to happen next. Some actions are routine and I understand what is required, but others are always changing.

If things became really bad and I suffer what I call a sensory overload, then I close out all the sounds and noises of the world. I could sit somewhere quietly or put my hands over my ears and enjoy the quieter sounds of life. Somehow to just sit and close off gives me space and time to recover from being anxious. It helps me to calm down. If I cannot find the room to do this, then the overload can build to an explosion!

In November 1995 I went into overload. I covered my ears, walked around in circles and then the screams came up from within me. I walked out of the lounge room, through the corridor and into the bedroom. There was no way out. I simply created one by attempting to walk through the closed bedroom window. The window cracked along one side. I just had to get away from expectation. I had attempted too much during the day and had not recognised the signs of sensory overload. Fortunately, I was not on my own and the words and actions of a good friend enabled me to go to bed and sleep.

•

LIFE

Dark and dense speckled with the inevitable light of
　　the season's sun.
I wish that you could be here. We have so much to
　　share, so little in common.
The rain falling steadily at daybreak, meaning to wake
　　the sleepy spiders and remind the blackbird of his
　　long lost song.
Puddles, murky and solemn, like cold porridge on a
　　winter's day.
Sometimes it's hard to remember when you are
　　feeling far away, just what was it like when
　　children use to play?

101

Where there are no interruptions, life goes on. The
music and light shown within my head could hum
and buzz a reassuring rhythm.

•

For reasons I do not understand, everyday decisions can be
very traumatic. As a child, everyday occurrences could be
very frightening.

To help with these decisions, I had favourite clothes to
wear, favourite eating utensils and a habitual, structured
routine. Of course, there were times when this structure
came apart at the seams and bedlam occurred. When this
happened, I experienced a feeling of terror and insecurity.
Distress and emotional chaos followed thus. To regain
myself, I would talk out loud, pace up and down, flap my
hands and try to focus on something familiar. At times, I
could hum or sing softly to myself. This acted as a
distraction and the fear inside me lessened.

As I grew older, I learnt to listen to the talk in my head.
This usually took place quietly, but sometimes the words
spoken out loud were more helpful. Today, I usually have
some soft material in a pocket that I can run my fingers
over to gain reassurance. Occasionally, I enjoy sitting in the
bedroom cupboard, closing off from all outside
disturbances. I also have a good friend, Ruth, who knows
how life can affect me. Ruth has the ability to calm me
down and help me to get life back into perspective. That is,
other people's perspective, which is called normal and is
apparently free from confusion and fear.

When I do not have a good friend with me and I am in
such a difficult situation, then I use the telephone. Words

have always helped me to form the bigger picture. When they are out there in the airwaves I can see better and this helps me to relax.

I know that at times I have caused people to move away. I tell stories that friends have heard so many times before, but it is the repetition that builds the picture that helps me to understand what is happening.

A psychologist once explained to me that learning could be enhanced by the use of certain strategies. He said that these strategies would help me to put emphasis over certain formations to create patterns. These patterns could aid and assist in the making of socially appropriate responses to various situations. Perhaps it is better explained when likened to the forming and practising of new or desirable habits.

The goal is the new behaviour but the strategy is what takes you there. He suggested that I watch and observe people in everyday situations so I could learn their patterns of responding and then think about strategies for my own learning. For me to grasp this in a practical way, I studied people and their interactions by watching them on television, in trams, buses and trains and in just about every situation I could, without upsetting anyone.

•

SPACE AND TIME

Rooms, rooms and more rooms, all filled with spaces
and faces.
Some stand up and some sit down, others lie or just
move around.
No one is right and no one is wrong.
Words that are spoken are heard and then gone.
Time is important and then it is not, it was for a
moment, but then I forgot.
So I write all this down and I just hang around,
looking and watching and listening to sound.
Please be clear, and say it like it is, then I will hear
you and understand what this means.

•

Chapter 13

The Anguish Of Change

My excitement over those things that move me is always constant. Every year I look forward to certain events and happenings with great anticipation and excruciating tension — it's so hard to wait! My responses to life are always the same. I am so predictable that it's hard for me to understand why someone gets bored with enjoying a certain pleasure.

In the film *What's Eating Gilbert Grape?* the teenage autistic boy, Arnie, was terribly excited every year when the caravans passed along the road near his home for the summer holidays. This event, so mundane to other folk, made him ecstatic and his excitement could not be contained. This is my experience with so many of life's events that thrill me. It is also true to say that my disappointment, frustration and fear levels are as extreme — and as constant.

One morning in 1995 I was sitting with a friend and sharing morning tea when she told me about her feelings about Christmas and family. The expectations upon her robbed her of any joy or motivation to celebrate. The anxiety and tension was interfering with her sleep patterns, appetite and enthusiasm for life. Her words surprised me because I had assumed that everyone was excited, just like me. I love Christmas — the glitter, colour, spectacle, carols by candlelight, and the opportunity for adventure.

I have always known that for many, Christmas is a hard time, that isolation and depression increase when people are confronted with grief, poverty, and separation from loved ones. I found it very difficult to understand my friend though — her family loved and accepted her. Why was she so depressed?

·

Just as I hold on to things that excite me, the terror of change and separation is all-consuming. Sucking the roof of my mouth or being calmed down by the person who loves me are my main routes to peace again.

Other calming activities, such as being alone in an empty room, listening to easy music or using a relaxation technique are also helpful.

The best strategy is to prepare an autistic person before the intended change occurs.

·

Change, change and more change
Of context, place and time.
Why is it that life's transient stage
Plays havoc with my mind?

You said, "We'll go to McDonald's"
But this was just a thought.
I was set for hours,
But the plan then came to nought.

My tears and confused frustration,
At plans that do not appear,
Are painful beyond recognition
And push me deeper into fear.

How can life be so determined?
How can change be so complete?
With continuity there is no end.
Security and trust are sweet.

So, who said that change would not hurt me?
Who said my "being" could not be safe?
Change said, "You need continuity
In order to find your place."

For change makes all things different.
They no longer are the same.
What was it that you really meant?
All I feel is the pain.

•

It's very hard to learn the lesson that things don't and can't
last forever. Something that has taken me a very long time
to grasp is the idea of mortality. I am always surprised when
something comes to an end. This is true in relation to
special outings, holidays, shop leases, friendships, semesters
at school, seasons of the year, blossoms on the fruit trees or
just a wet windy day.

Sometimes my surprise can turn to sadness or even terror.
While the event is occurring I feel part of it, but when it
ceases then I cease to be too.

When I was a child of two, I sat under our round living-
room table during a storm. I did this because the floor was
beneath my body and the table over it. This gave me a sense
of myself as being separate from the thunder and I felt safe.
If I left the safety of the table, then I feared the thunder
would scoop me up and I might be lost in its roar. Even

after the storm passed, I stayed beneath the table. It took me the rest of the day before I would venture out.

I think this was the case, because I was surprised the storm was over. It was hard to trust that it had really gone – I mean, how can something be there for a moment or longer, and then not there any more?

To some degree, I still experience these feelings and thoughts today. I no longer feel the need to hide beneath a table during a storm, but I still experience a sense of surprise and wonder when the storm has passed.

Some people I know experience mood changes and their emotions towards life and other people differ from time to time. But if I was excited to meet a certain situation or person, then that is how I would feel each time it occurred. This is also true for fear and apprehension, of course. Once I have felt afraid, I tend to always fear that situation or person. It's very difficult to alter my mind.

I have noticed that other people do not seem surprised or too upset by change. They may comment "that's life" or "you can have too much of a good thing" or "variety is the spice of life". These comments, I think, are meant to make everything okay again. Maybe they say these things so that they will not have to experience trauma or displeasure? Their comments do not really make any sense to me. I have tried so hard to understand them, I have said the words over and over to myself, but they sound empty and hollow..

•

A Point to Ponder

As far as possible, I will keep some parts of a situation before change occurs, and take them with me into the change. This way, the change is felt as less powerful and I am still in control. For example, I might choose to wear my leather and canvas runners and my red socks, even though the weather forecast is 30°C. At other times, I wear my woollen hat, even though the occasion is not suitable for it.

I once had a really special hat. It was purple on the outside and had a red lining. I wore it on the aeroplane when we travelled to England and even though it was a summer hat I wore it in the snow. I was very upset when it got left behind at my sister's place and felt really scared without it. It was as if that hat was part of me – without it I felt a sense of separation and fear. I know these emotions are illogical – a hat cannot make me safe on a plane – but I cried for ages when I realised it was missing.

A mother of an autistic 12 year old boy once asked me why her son screamed when the railing he had been following and holding onto came to an end. I tried to explain this same concept: the concept of familiarity and change, of gaining a sense of security and of self, as perceived through the railings. I gain these emotions by touching inanimate objects or something with continuity, like railings, wearing my hat and feeling the definition on my head, or by being held firmly by my friend.

Chapter 14

Finding Love And Friendship

Why is it that someone can say they want to get to know you, share their lives with you, and then pull away when you disappoint them or become too demanding?

I believe this is a question with which many autistic people battle. For us, it is much more helpful to be told when we are causing someone's space to feel invaded, or when we are being insensitive. I can deal with what I know — it's what I don't know that causes me the most pain.

I have been told, "what you don't know won't hurt you," but boundaries, rules, regulations and concrete structure provide understanding, and therefore enable an appropriate response. We do not need lengthy explanations about the whys and wherefores of life. In fact, if you try to go into detail with an autistic person, they will probably leave you talking to yourself, while their attention is caught away by a passing butterfly!

It is always risky to love someone and allow them to love you, but it is a risk worth taking. I do not like the discomfort I feel when those I love are disappointed or unhappy with me. There are times when my behaviour is seen as bizarre and embarrassing. This makes me sad and depressed. I keep working on these things, in the hope they will decrease and my friends who know me will see beyond my idiosyncrasies and just love Wendy!

The following dichotomy is very interesting to me: There are times when I am in "professional" mode and the person

I am with would probably never believe I was autistic. They might think I am younger than I am or a little eccentric but otherwise perfectly "normal".

I felt really mystified by this and so I talked to my friend, Ruth. She explained that we are all different with different people.

"Some of us even have 'telephone voices' that we employ when we speak over the telephone." I didn't get it.

"How can I know who I am if I am different people at different times?"

"Well, it's not that you are different people, but rather that different aspects of Wendy, the same person, are revealed at different times and with different individuals."

Her response opened another concept for me. My confusion lessened each time this happened and as Ruth continues with me today, I know I will keep "growing up". Becoming more adult and less child-like is quite a challenge and one I am glad I do not have to attempt alone.

●

MY LOVE

It wasn't always this way.
The joy of knowing you and sharing in your life has
    taught me that I am able to love myself.
In your presence, I come to life in a way that I have
    never experienced before.
The rag doll, who is losing her stuffing, becomes the
    musical clown, so full of colour and vitality.

You set me free from the demands of self-
introspection and its ugly forest of gloom.
In its place I am able to walk through sunlit woods
and enjoy choruses of birdsong.

Your smile delights my eyes and the peace in my soul
rolls over me, like the gentle waves of a calm
ocean.
So soothing is your voice to my ears, that even the
roar of my lions within cannot shatter it.

Thank you, my love, for your quiet assurance and
humble vulnerability — to you I owe a never-
ending debt, my life.

•

"I am not an idiot," I said, as the person talking to me repeated their comments. I was feeling particularly sensitive at that time and fed up with being treated as if I was stupid. As far back as I can remember, this has been my experience. "What do I have to do or what must I become before other people afford me the same respect they demand for themselves?"

So often it appears to me that people don't take me seriously. Do they believe that either I won't notice, won't feel hurt, or I'm just not worth respecting? This is the attitude I meet often, especially among professionals. It is the one thing that is guaranteed to make me angry and at times I just can't be bothered fighting it. I used to fight but it's so much easier to just get tired and withdraw.

It is true that I don't always get the joke or understand the scenario. Sometimes simple instructions can be confusing to me and I need them broken down into smaller chunks, and written down. However, I'm not stupid. When I went to the movies and heard Forest Gump say, "I know what love is", I could feel the lump in my throat tighten. "So do I," were the words that echoed in my head, "so do I."

In the past, skin contact was uncomfortable for me and I avoided it at all costs. Then, as time went by, I appeared to form strong attachments to certain individuals. I needed to be very close to them and was always needing them to hold or hug me. The stimulus of physical contact told me that I was okay and whenever one of these individuals could not be available to me, I moved into fear. Rocking myself and crying was my usual response; sometimes I would plead to be held and became very demanding.

I found it very hard to understand that certain physical contact was appropriate and some was not. It was also hard to understand the concept of "personal space". I always wanted my cuddles, irrespective of how the other person was feeling! I can only ask for understanding on this matter.

Of course, it's important to learn how to consider others, but all I could feel was my need. I still find it very difficult to put myself "in the other person's shoes". I can only feel my needs and myself — everything outside is foreign and alien to me. I operate at a relational level by habit, routine and strategy. I do know what it is to be misunderstood or to suffer injustice; I do have feelings. It's just that I feel and express them differently to most other people and my world is egocentric.

Sometimes I think I feel more deeply than most people, and I wish I could turn the feeling off.

When a dog looks into the face of a human being, its desire is for some kind of attention. It may want food, a walk or some affection. When it is tired, it simply lies down to sleep. It feels no need to say "good night" or "if it's okay by you I will do this or that". A dog is constant, loyal, and always on your side. Even when its needs are not met or are misunderstood it appears to bear no grudge. I like dogs.

Chapter 15

It's My World Too

Things can happen that inspire me to "keep trying". Once I was walking back from an early breakfast at McDonald's. At 6.30am it was already 28°C. Glancing at the ground as I walked along, I noticed some movement at my feet and saw the last exit moments of a cicada crawling out of a hole in the ground. I watched this creature transform before my eyes from a dull brownish-green bug into a beautiful bright green and gold, singing creation. The process took only one and a half hours.

Apparently this large larvae spends seven years underground. I understand now why it needs to sing so loudly when it grows its wings! I was so excited to catch this experience and be in on this creature's birth. Many people passed by and I told them the cicada story. One neighbour was passing by in her motor car when she saw me looking up into the tree and flapping my hands with excitement. She stopped and came over.

She thought maybe I needed help or my cat was stuck up the tree. When I told her what I was doing she looked at me in amazement and smiled, then said that she had to go to the garage. I have since heard that people thought my standing in the heat for one and a half hours to watch an insect was a crazy thing to do. I think it is they who are crazy. By choosing not to stand and watch, they missed out on sharing an experience that was so beautiful and exhilarating. A miracle can be happening all around us and no one is aware of it.

I know how it feels to be underground, trapped in a silence that vibrates only more silence. I also know the joy of the moments when I have been able to break through the silence and life has made sense to me — when light and colour form a picture that has inspired me and I have caught a train, or ridden a tram or eaten breakfast at McDonald's.

In the past few years, I have begun to realise that my outlook on life is vastly different to that of most other people. I had always assumed everyone operated as I did, and felt about things as I do. Intellectually, I realised that people are individual and different, but it has only just occurred to me *how* extensive is that difference.

Over the years, I usually tried to contain my excitement and joy over life's happenings and watched to see what makes other people happy or sad. If they laughed or were unmoved, then this was my signal that it was all right for me to do likewise. This process was hard work and although it helped me to be more observant of others, it robbed me of spontaneity and enjoyment of the richness of my own experience.

Today the recognition of this fact has freed me in many ways and I now allow myself the choice. In most situations my excitement and enjoyment of life is spontaneous and unaffected by the responses of others. The need for acceptance and friendship with other people is still quite real but it does not dominate my interactions with them. It is truly wonderful to be enjoying the discovery of self and of others so that differentiation of needs, wants and of rights can be understood.

My friend Lesley told me you need to know that you have rights before they can be explored. Her words made sense to me. It was as if a light came on and the reality of the scene before me was clearer.

"Why does it have to be so difficult?" The words left my mouth rather loudly and a friend who had joined me for coffee jumped in surprise.

"What's so difficult?" she asked.

"Everything!" I did not want to try to explain.

Today my understanding of most things is very good. I know I am valuable and have a place in the world. I have become my own person and truly like who I am. The process has been a difficult one and I know that my being egocentric is just too much for some people. How much more comfortable humans are with those of us who conform to expectation, who fit in with conventional "norms" and who are not an embarrassment.

The good news is that I too have learnt to "blend in" and much of the time you would not notice me or give me a second glance. I am also able to say that being autistic has its challenges, these are what have enabled me to share my story with you. My adventure is not finished yet!

•

A Point to Ponder

There are many more experiences to decipher and decode. My life is seriously taking on a new perspective — one I aim to use as my guide for the future and my reflection for the past. I will never "grow out" of being autistic but I hope that many more people will understand autism better because they have read this book.

•

"You'd think the buses would run on time"
The lady says out loud.
"You mark my words, it will be fine,"
The man yells from the crowd.
I stared at each, in disbelief,
What is it that they mean?

The words we use to speak each day,
Should say the things we need to say.
But when in doubt I'll leave it out
And choose instead another way.

•

Lightning Source UK Ltd.
Milton Keynes UK
10 December 2010

164183UK00002B/9/P

9 781853 029110